ENERGY, JUSTICE

Energy, Justice, AND Peace

A Reflection on Energy in the Current Context of Development and Environmental Protection

Pontifical Council for Justice and Peace

PREFACE BY
Peter K. A. Cardinal Turkson and Mario Toso

Paulist Press
New York / Mahwah, NJ

Cover image by jannoon028/shutterstock.com
Cover design by Joe Gallagher
Book design by Lynn Else

Library of Congress Control Number: 2015959808

ISBN 978-0-8091-4985-8 (paperback)
ISBN 978-1-58768-606-1 (e-book)

Published by Paulist Press in 2016
997 Macarthur Boulevard
Mahwah, New Jersey 07430

www.paulistpress.com

Printed and bound in the
United States of America

Contents

CONTENTS

Contents

CONTENTS

Contents

Preface

During the first decade of the new millennium, growing attention has been directed to several issues related to the deterioration of the environment, such as the economic crisis on a national and international level, the tendency to the exhaustion of natural resources, and food insecurity. Similar phenomena, which increasingly affect our planet and the whole mankind, do not seem to be heading toward a quick solution without an adequate widespread awareness of their seriousness and a strong mobilization of civil societies and public institutions on a national and international scale. By this contribution to reflection, the Pontifical Council for Justice and Peace intends, in particular, to draw attention to the multiple interactions of *energy* with the above-listed issues. They imply evident problems of *justice*, which jeopardize the precious gift of *peace*. Indeed, the inequality in the availability of and access to energy causes a fracture that separates privileged areas from unprivileged ones more and more radically, to the detriment of a sustainable and equitable development for all. It should be noted that in various countries, supply shortages and related financial transactions considerably affect the problem of hunger. Furthermore, in some cases the exploitation of sources and the production and transportation of energy trigger economic and political instability that may result in regional conflicts, which end up compromising global stability. It is a fact that certain modes of production and consumption have a strong impact on environment, economies, and societies.

We can reasonably think that the *energy challenges* that we are facing today undermine not only our ability to achieve the current development goals, but also the possibility to intelligently set new ones, with a view to a sustainable future. On the other hand, it should be remembered that—thanks to the technological and scientific achievements, the evolution of policies and objectives, as well as the global concern about a real sustainable, integral, and solidarity-based development, and above all thanks to the understanding and assumption of responsibility by current societies—energy becomes a strategic element toward the solution of the abovementioned issues.

For this reason, this easy-to-read instrument is meant to focus on the relationship of energy with justice and peace, by showing how unresolved energy issues may pose a serious threat to these essential goods and also by examining how energy may contribute to a real, integral, and sustainable development.

The Pontifical Council wishes to propose an interpretation of the issues under consideration, starting from its specific ethical-religious competence, which is also that of the universal Church. This contribution is bound neither to a particular historical-technological context nor to events dedicated to energy and development, organized by international institutions. Its purpose is to provide a general reflection on these issues, starting, as far as possible, from a biblical-theological vision, with the help of the judgment principles and criteria and practical guidelines offered by the Church's social doctrine or teaching.

In a 2008 speech to the members of the General Assembly of the United Nations, Benedict XVI reminded us that the "protection of the environment, of resources and of the climate, require all international leaders to act jointly and to show a readiness to work in good faith, respecting the law, and promoting solidarity with the weakest regions of the planet."[1] Even a proper and effective management of energy requires a commitment of responsibility, so that neither the hope for a better future, nor the respect for human dignity, nor the ability to choose good will ever vanish. This responsibility, commensurate with the issues under discussion, is a global one. In fact, it "is concerned not just with energy but with the whole of creation, which must not be bequeathed to future generations depleted of its resources."[2]

PETER K. A. Card. TURKSON, *President*
+ MARIO TOSO, *Secretary*

CHAPTER 1

Introduction

1. The Interest of the Church in the Energy Question

As pointed out in *Centesimus annus* by Saint John Paul II, the Catholic Church, by the very nature of its ethical-religious competence, has "something to say about specific human situations, both individual and communal, national and international. She formulates a genuine doctrine for these situations, a *corpus* which enables her to analyze social realities, to make judgments about them and to indicate directions to be taken for the just resolution of the problems involved."[1] Especially from Paul VI onward, the Church has been particularly interested in the question of integral development of peoples. Being a primary factor thereof, energy is the subject of discussions and reflections that are underway at various institutions responsible for analyzing and managing development-related issues on a national and international level.

The Social Doctrine of the Church cannot consider development as only a synonym of technical-technological progress or as a mere economic evolution, characterized by increasing consumption possibilities or production indices. The Church emphasizes the need for "a fuller and more nuanced concept of development,"[2] which can be offered by a *full-fledged humanism*. A fully human development is essential to enhance the respect for every individual's dignity and creativity, "his capacity to respond to his personal vocation, and thus to God's call."[3] It is therefore necessary to aim for a global development that embraces all the constitutive dimensions of man.[4] The

1

Church, by its very nature and foundation, addresses the issue of the development of peoples with Christ's charity, inviting us to cooperate with all our heart and all our intelligence.[5] Hence, it is clear that, in many respects, energy is—as will be seen in the first part of the text—a challenge for justice and peace. The energy question, often referred to by John Paul II and Benedict XVI in their addresses and writings, is undoubtedly among the *signs of the times*, which should be assumed, read, and interpreted in the light of the wisdom of the Gospel. These reflections are just meant to follow the path of social discernment rooted in the experience of faith, which puts us in constant communion with God and his work of salvation. This discernment also puts us in communion with the whole humanity that the Church intends to serve. And this communion is what allows us to draw upon a broader knowledge than the merely human one and to formulate a cultural synthesis constitutively open to the transcendent dimension of existence. It does not obviate the consideration of material goods and technical problems. On the contrary, it sheds light on them and places them in a theological, anthropological, and ethical framework that enables us to evaluate them and target their use according to a broader human and cultural significance.

In the light of a discernment that places energy and issues related thereto in a context of revelation and redemption, the reflections of the Pontifical Council are meant to highlight the following key aspects for its management.

- Energy, in its many forms, is a gift of God, made freely available to the whole humanity. Therefore, its hoarding or exclusive use by a few is not legitimate. The Creator, through his infinite love, causes the sun to rise on all, the evil and the good, wherever they live.[6] Everyone, then, is called to act in the same spirit and to work to ensure the universal destination of energy, granting lighting for those who are in the dark, heating for those who are cold, and providing the necessary energy to prepare food for those who are hungry.[7]

Gratuitousness, discussed in *Caritas in veritate*, should contribute to the solidarity-based management of this precious gift.[8]

- Energy is an *ability-to-do*, entrusted by God to human beings as an extension of their skills. It belongs by its very nature to such skills whereby He allows the human being to implement the commandment to cultivate and keep creation:[9] man is placed in the garden to work and take care of it, and this activity makes him similar to his Creator.[10] By entrusting man with this extremely high task, God urges him to act upon freedom and responsibility. Energy, the fruit of creation, is a tool entrusted to man for collective and solidarity-based growth. It must be understood, therefore, in the light of the dimension of both *know-how* (technique) and the purposes of our *action* (ethics). The ethical question about energy and its use does not exclude the energy question, but it is, in a way, a constitutive element of its essence.

- Human activities related to energy need to be guided by a thorough and competent knowledge of its nature, as well as by a demanding moral and social responsibility: creation, including energy resources, must be known in its fundamental laws and potentials. Reflection enlightened by faith is aware that created things enjoy their own laws and values which must be gradually deciphered, put to use, and regulated by men.[11] Only the sincere and honest search and sharing of these competences will enable individuals and social groups to use energy in a fair way. Therefore, energy also requires a mutual exchange of responsible training and information by men and by the different generations.

- Creation has its own goodness and proper perfection, but it did not spring forth complete from the hands of

3

the Creator. It was created *in a state of journeying* toward an ultimate yet to be attained, to which God has destined it.[12] Human activities related to energy, in view of this dimension, must be driven by an eschatological awareness and be guided by a series of teleological reflections, which stretch far beyond the mere technical and instrumental rationality. Pope Francis points out that "the gaze of science thus benefits from faith: faith encourages the scientist to remain constantly open to reality in all its inexhaustible richness. Faith awakens the critical sense by preventing research from being satisfied with its own formulae and helps it to realize that nature is always greater. By stimulating wonder before the profound mystery of creation, faith broadens the horizons of reason to shed greater light on the world which discloses itself to scientific investigation."[13]

• Moreover, since the abovementioned activities are carried out by people—that is, free and responsible beings, who are however subject to selfish inclinations and to evil[14]—they need purification and permanent redemption offered by Jesus Christ. In fact, creation suffers because humanity does not yet live the *novelty of Easter*, and so we are witnessing its continuous spoliation, due to the violence perpetrated by individuals and societies.

• The communion with Jesus Christ, the New Adam, allows experiencing the commitments related to energy with a view to achieving integral, solidarity-based, sustainable development open to Transcendence. It allows, in other words, living according to such global rationality, universal fraternity, and rectitude of life as proposed by *Caritas in veritate*.[15] Thus, as this encyclical teaches, we must implement in social dynamics the transition from the predominant perspective of individuals

4

to that of communion, from the perspective of groups to that of a global human family. This transition is not easy, because it requires a radical change in mentality, based on *fraternity* and *solidarity*, always loved and pursued.

- From the point of view of energy, today's conditions supporting the common good of human family entail the establishment of effective global governance. Global institutions must correspond to the equally global problems, as we will better see later.

Leaning on a similar platform of wisdom, which places human activity in the mystery of experienced and lived salvation, and makes us sharers of the "new creation"[16] initiated by Jesus Christ through his incarnation, death, and resurrection, the reflections of the Pontifical Council intend to achieve the following objectives:

1. to help to set the energy question within a wider vision of development, shelving sectorially limited analyses and lines of argument that only pursue technical-economic feasibility and disregard solidarity and justice;
2. to show how some policies and approaches to the energy question prove unsustainable, because they generate underdevelopment, conflicts, environmental deterioration, economic unbalances, and injustices on a large scale;
3. to further show that energy can, and therefore must, be managed as a *key factor* for development and peace;
4. to provide judgment principles and criteria accessible to all, along with some concrete proposals for the harmonious management of energy.

In this context, it is important to bear in mind that the Church is experiencing the theme of ecumenism with increasing intensity.

Therefore, in the ripples of the "Year of Faith" proclaimed by Benedict XVI, the concern of ecumenical dialogue over the relationship between energy, justice, and peace appears to be particularly relevant. This dialogue is not solely aimed at pursuing convergence of religious faith, but also at contributing to the implementation of good practices. In this way, dialogue among religions can usefully be articulated and completed, dealing with concrete problems of coexistence, and living a shared responsibility for society and the whole humanity.[17]

2. Remembering the Role of Humanity in Relation to Creation

The Holy Scriptures state that God is the Creator and Lord of the world and what it contains. All this is entrusted to man so that he lives there and uses it responsibly, not only for himself, but also for his brothers.[18] Every human being, "created to God's image, received [a mandate] to govern the world with justice and holiness."[19] Humanity must absolutely become aware of its role: every person must strive to manage and take care of the planet the same way a good administrator would, knowing that he is neither the lord nor the creator of it, but just one of those to whom the earth has been entrusted temporarily. God wishes to let the entire human family share His own solicitude. Nature must not only be preserved, but also made to flourish in its beauty and usefulness, and managed responsibly with the same love that God nourishes for it and for all of his children.[20] The concept of *service* then becomes the key to understand how to lead our life in the created world. This is undoubtedly a greatly ennobling task whose perspective also regards the relationship between man and energy. This broader understanding helps to resolutely overcome two possible ambiguities: that man thinks of himself as the absolute lord of the earth and that he considers his relationship with creation as an abstract concept, mistaking passive preservation of the existing with respect for nature. We must be true to the ideal of a balanced relationship, in which creation is experienced as the dwelling that God entrusts to us and as a gift that must be nurtured and enhanced for future generations.

As explained by Benedict XVI, this entails the "responsible stewardship over nature, in order to protect it, to enjoy its fruits and to cultivate it in new ways, with the assistance of advanced technologies, so that it can worthily accommodate and feed the world's population."[21]

Likewise, Pope Francis has urged all those who have positions of responsibility and all men and women of goodwill to be "protectors," in a creative and responsible sense, of each other, of the environment, and of God's plan inscribed in nature.[22]

Paul VI already pointed out the behavior that should distinguish not only a scientist, a technician, and a politician, but also every person: everyone must sincerely wonder about the earthly future of humanity and responsibly contribute to prepare it, preserving current worldly goods and eliminating the risks posed by erroneous human choices. The Pope considered this solidarity with future generations a form of charity to which many, however, are sensitive today in the framework of ecology.[23]

3. Explanation of Terms

Before proceeding with the description and analysis of the issues of our times, it is useful to provide a brief but essential *explicatio terminorum*, in order to define the scope and understand the significance of the goods at stake.

Energy

The word *energy* derives from Late Latin *energīa*, which in turn refers to Greek ἐνέργεια (*enérgheia*), consisting of the intensifying particle *en*, and *érgon*, the work performed. The term, which was also extended to other meanings, was coined by Aristotle, especially to indicate the *actual force that makes movement and action*, and that is different from pure potentiality or virtuality, and from privation or nothing.[24]

The concept of energy is not a primary concept, as it presupposes that of work, or the use of a force to generate a movement. Energy can therefore be defined as the ability of a system to perform a task. For example: the implementation of the force necessary to lift a weight is directly related to the energy that the system has to perform that action. In modern physics, energy can be defined as the *ability of a body or of a system to make an effort*. The extent of this effort—to emit heat or to make a movement—is in turn the extent of energy.

It is important to understand that energy occurs in many forms, different from each other, such as: thermal energy for heating, which is obtained either directly from the sun or from the soil, or through the use of fuels; kinetic energy, which, present in wind or water, is turned into mechanical energy through a wind blade or a turbine, is immediately converted into electrical energy in a generator and, after being distributed through the grid, reconverted into several forms (light energy, mechanical energy again, thermal energy, etc.).

A fundamental concept to be taken into account to fully understand all the issues that will be explained herein is that energy can neither be created nor destroyed, but it is continuously transformed. Each of these transformations, however, involves a *loss*, which actually consists of the portion of energy that can no longer be used (*principle of entropy*). This assumption underlies the concept of *transformation efficiency*, which is of great significance in the discussion on the issue of energy. It is exactly this inevitable energy *loss* that confirms the centrality of ethics. Energy transformations are never *ethically neutral* activities. As a result of a certain degree of irreversibility, they herald questions about the meaning and the purposes, which require numerous competences in order to be responsibly addressed.

Finally, from a social-economic point of view, the concept of energy refers to both the *natural energy resource* and its *product intended for consumption.* For example: calories contained in food and the movement of the human body guaranteed by them; the wind and the wind power that it generates; crude oil and thermal or mechanical energy and electricity obtained therefrom.

Energy Sources

Energy sources are those *energy stores* from which it is distributed for use. Sources are divided into *primary* and *secondary.*

Primary sources are directly available in nature (coal, crude oil, gas, water, sun, wind, etc.) and therefore do not result from transformations of other forms of energy. These sources are also distinguished in terms of both their available quantity and the time necessary for their regeneration. *Secondary* energy sources require further transformations in order to be used by end users. Among them, we can mention petrol or diesel obtained from petroleum, electrical power produced by technological devices that consume primary sources.

In order to be used, a source of energy must have certain peculiar characteristics of:

- concentration: it must be possible to concentrate the source of energy within a relatively limited area (a power plant, a tank, a field, etc.);
- direction: it must be possible to direct the product (petrol, water, sun rays) to the plant where it is to be used (burner, turbine, reflector, lens, mirror);
- fractionation: it must be possible to fractionate the source, in order to use only the part, whether large or small, necessary at that moment;
- continuity: the source must be able to function for some time, providing its energy without interruptions if possible, and it must not run out in a few seconds. There are many examples of considerable quantities of energy concentrated in a very short time (lightning, an explosion, the falling of any object): of course, these

types of energy cannot be used for civil or industrial purposes;[25]
- regulation: it must be possible to scale the energy provided by the source as needed.

Each source can be described according to these characteristics: the better they are, the more valuable it will be.[26] At present, the secondary source that we call *electrical energy* seems to meet the above requirements ever better than any other, and this is the reason for its success and widespread distribution.

The development of new sources of energy causes the obsolescence of previous specific technologies and skills, and requires the design of new infrastructure and the readjustment of the labor market to the new industrial capacities, sometimes triggering more or less temporary unemployment flows. These characteristics indicate that the energy sources available are indissolubly linked with the development of man, society, and culture. In short, the concept of energy being a secondary concept, in order to highlight the related ethical implications, one should always consider the primary reference from which it draws its meaning and importance: the person and his or her integral promotion. It would be absolutely wrong to assume that energy sources and their use are morally neutral elements, which do not have within them an inescapable call to the exercise of morality, understood as an experience of freedom and responsibility.

Renewable and Non-renewable Energy

It is worth explaining the difference between *renewable* and *non-renewable* energy resources.

The former can be found in nature in apparently unlimited quantities: the sun, the sea waves, the wind, the heat of the earth (geothermal energy). Besides them, we should mention those *biomasses* (or *bioenergy*) on which we can draw as if they were renewable, taking care of their regeneration on a human timescale. Bioenergy means those materials of biological origin, which may serve as a source of energy and among which the most common is wood. We can also consider an animal's plowing, carrying, or towing as renewable energy.

By non-renewable or exhaustible energy resources, on the contrary, we mainly and commonly mean fossil fuels, such as coal, oil, and gas. These fuels—regardless of the quantity currently available in the various fields—may become scarce and run out, since their natural regeneration time exceeds the human timescale, in the sense that it is very slow compared to the demand and consumption of the world's population. These resources—it is worth mentioning—still cover about 80% of the world energy production.[27] Even minerals like uranium and thorium, which are the basis of the production of nuclear energy, must be considered non-renewable.

Uses of Energy

Primary sources cannot be used directly by consumers. It is up to the energy industry, or to simple and more widespread devices, to turn them into secondary sources suited to the demands and to distribute them widely to users. The energy industries that perform this transformation through crude oil refineries and power plants, powered by fossil fuels or by renewable sources, distribute these secondary sources by means of pipelines, vehicles, electrical grids, or storage facilities. More simply, these devices use the same primary sources and distribute the product (e.g., electricity) at a local level. This is referred to as *distributed energy generation*.

End uses conventionally regard four different types of users:

- farming;
- manufacturing industry;
- civilian users (divided between domestic activities of residences and service production activities);
- transport.

End users use electricity and thermal secondary sources directly, but in most cases they have to convert them into other forms of energy, such as heat for air conditioning or mechanical energy for the operation of household appliances. This results, of course, in further transformation losses, even at end users.

Energy production means processing natural resources, and therefore it must take into account some considerations that frame the relationship between humans and the environment in a planetary system, recognized as living and evolving. This system entails dangers, that is, phenomena and processes, both natural and manmade, which might damage one or more groups of people, their possessions, and their environment, if no precautions are taken. The production of energy and its use is, therefore, inevitably fraught with dangers of various kinds.[28] One issue of particular importance occurs when the production of energy makes human communities vulnerable by exposing them to dangers. Vulnerability is the inability to stand up to danger or to respond to it with appropriate actions, when this turns into a disaster. Human communities may be subjected to several vulnerabilities stemming from the production of energy:

- *economic* vulnerabilities, which prevent groups of people from exposing to dangers, or impose them to do so, because they are unable, for example, to live elsewhere;
- *physical* vulnerabilities, related to the nature of the energy sources in question, to the territory, or to other characteristics of the transformation process.

The resulting risk is the probability for a danger to turn into a disaster. Vulnerability and dangers do not represent a risk in themselves when taken separately. On the contrary, they become a risk, or in other words, they increase the probability of a disaster, if contemplated jointly. However, risks can be reduced or managed if cultures and policies are created to protect people and the environment in energy transformation processes, and if communities are made aware of their vulnerability to the existing dangers. It is necessary to create a culture which can take steps to ensure that the dangers related to the production, processing, and use of energy do not turn into disasters.

Energy Reserves

The concept of *reserve* defines the available quantity of a natural resource, verified by surveys and studies, which can be exploited economically by man through the technologies in hand. Only a portion of the existing natural resources is, therefore, defined as a reserve. Moreover, in consideration of technological and scientific development, the same reserve can be reduced or increased. Three basic elements help to define the concept of reserve:

- the existing technology, which can extract and process the natural resource;
- the market, which is able, from the economic point of view, to set a value and to measure the convenience of extraction and processing, when these costs are less than earnings;
- the political or military considerations of nation states or transnational organizations about the possibility or strategic advisability of the extraction, processing, or distribution of energy resources.

When extraction and processing costs exceed earnings, they might discourage the use of energy sources with the existing technologies. This situation, however, might be overcome in the future. In these cases, we are talking about *reserves in the broader sense* or *potential reserves for the future*. As already mentioned, the reserves of a natural resource are not constant, but they vary due to several factors. Over time, technological innovations tend to solve technical problems related to extraction, to reduce their costs, and to lead to the discovery of new deposits. On the other hand, future market conditions or any geopolitical tensions may generate such an increase in the price of raw materials as to make it advantageous to exploit deposits, which was previously considered to be uneconomic.

Energy Question

Being a coalescence of several geopolitical concerns, the term *energy question* demands an interdisciplinary approach. This is because the various problems pertaining to energy are sometimes interconnected, as well as being simultaneous. Below is a partial list of these problems:

- pollution, resulting from the extraction and use of fossil fuels;
- the possible impact of emissions resulting from the production and consumption of energy on health, the climate, and the environment in general;
- the reduction of the possible environmental damage resulting from the use of energy, specified in the two points above;
- the effects of the price volatility of fossil energy and its scarcity on food source security and on the possibility of access by mankind;
- the uneasiness resulting from the gap between the growing demand of certain energy sources and the limited resources available;
- the search for indicators and criteria of reliability, aimed at setting up new systems based on the use of renewable energy;
- the effect of the lack of energy on development delays;
- the awareness that energy can generate conflicts in production sites and transit zones;
- the unjust and unequal sharing of energy resources and of the sale proceeds;
- the economically sustainable supply of the amount of

energy required by each country, so as to ensure its development;
- the widespread access to increasingly better forms of energy, technology, and research results, specifically related to:
  - the procedures for coordination between countries, to better target research, not to dissipate the public and private capital employed, to share scientific discoveries and their applications;
  - the access by the largest possible number of people to the most suitable technologies for their standard of living.

Energy Efficiency

Energy efficiency generally refers to an objective being pursued to achieve the same result with a smaller amount of energy. The adoption of energy-efficient cooking systems and the improvement of home insulation are examples of precautions allowing the achievement of the desired outcome (food preparation and heating) with a lower energy consumption.

Technology, especially if applied to transformation and transport processes, plays an important role in promoting energy efficiency, as its evolution ensures increasingly better results starting from the same quantity of resources.

For example: more and more electricity from the water flowing into the turbines of a hydroelectric power plant, or from the same quantity of uranium that powers a nuclear power plant; more and more kilometers covered by a vehicle with a liter of fuel; increasing output for every hour of sun exposure of a solar panel; more and more kilowatts available, thanks to the reduction of losses during transportation or the conversion from energy resource into usable energy.

Energy efficiency is an important goal since all processes related to the production of energy—from sources to consumption—may adversely affect societies, the various economies, and the environment. It then becomes a key factor in contexts characterized by scarcity and high cost of energy resources, especially with a view to optimizing the use of resources and reducing its environmental impact.

Distributed Generation

Distributed generation generally means production of energy through small systems designed for small local-scale consumption, such as a small generator that supplies electricity to an apparatus, a house, or a village. In certain contexts, this type of generation ensures the reduction of energy transportation costs and losses, and giving considerable responsibility to users as well. The term *off-grid*, which refers to not being connected to a large distribution network while producing and consuming energy on a local level, is emblematic of this approach.[29]

Energy-Related Activities

The energy production and utilization cycle involves the development of a number of concurrent activities: extraction, production, transportation, processing, storage, and distribution. These may vary according to the various forms of energy, but they still require the development of a complex system, whose operation may affect the population's access to energy.

4. Energy and Development: A Historical Reading

Energy and Development in the History of Humanity

It is worth recalling briefly the essential role of energy in human life and its progress in general. Throughout his history, "man has developed the forms of energy that he needed."[30] It is known that development was favored above all by those societies which, because of their scientific and cultural evolution, have been able to gain access over time to new and better forms of energy. The *search for energy*, which began in prehistoric times and is still ongoing, appears to be connected to the need for food and the hope to improve living conditions.[31] In ancient times, nature provided energy for human beings. The power to plow, grind, and carry was, indeed, offered by tame animals.[32] The fuel for food preparation, lighting, and craft activities was largely obtained from wood. Subsequently, energy provided a great impetus to industrial development. Technology and the exploitation of various natural resources have gradually brought about the transition from water mills to the steam engine, from hydroelectric power plants to nuclear ones, from coal-fired power plants to wind generators and solar panels. These are just a few examples of the energy mix that humanity has experienced throughout its constant progress.

Energy and Human Progress

While energy availability is clearly related to economic development, it is also correlated to *human progress* in the sense that human life can also be improved thanks to the increased energy availability *per capita*. This correlation is described by indicators which show that the increase in the availability of energy corresponds to an improvement of essential factors for the human condition, such as food availability, health, life expectancy, level of education, and culture.

Evolution of Energy Development Models

Until the seventeenth century, energy systems were based almost exclusively on the use of firewood to generate heat through distributed power plants, such as fireplaces in homes. In addition to wood, wind power and/or hydraulic power were used, though to a limited extent, to generate mechanical energy in centralized plants, such as mills and old factories. In the following centuries, the energy pattern gradually incorporated the use of fossil fuels (in historical order: coal, oil, and natural gas) and nuclear power. This led to the birth of the secondary sector, industry, besides the primary one, agriculture, as well as the consequent development of the industrial age and the further progressive evolution of economy toward the tertiary sector.

As a result of this evolution, the energy system of a developed country consists today of centralized or distributed power plants and network infrastructure. The whole thing is powered by a mix of renewable and non-renewable energy sources. This mix changes from one context to another, depending on various factors, such as presence of certain resources or possibility to import them, traditions, political choices, the orientation and advances of research, technological expertise, configuration of the territory, and population geography.

Thanks to the energy patterns developed and refined over the centuries, the most advanced countries are now able to ensure a high economic and social level for their populations. The energy system continues to evolve, in a gradual and progressive way, following the socio-technoeconomic development of each particular context.

The development of the energy industry, namely the availability of widely distributed secondary energy sources, has brought about a radical transformation of human society. Secondary sources have proved to be *general purpose* technologies, or technological instruments that have a high level of *technological pervasiveness*: once they are applied to a point of the production chain, their adoption and benefits spread rapidly upstream and downstream. Think of electric current: once introduced, its use has spread so much throughout the technological chain as to be omnipresent today. These social transformations generated by secondary energy sources have made the particular *anthropological density* of energy clear. Taking energy into account means looking upon man, his self-perception in history, and the possibilities for humanity to understand and increasingly fulfill his vocation to improvement. Every question about energy is, directly or indirectly, a question about man and his development.

5. Energy as an Indispensable Factor for Everybody

Energy is essential for development directed to the progress and improvement of the human condition. It is important for communities and nations, just as it is for the human body, with a view to its efficiency and autonomy. Without energy and strength, a body cannot move or act—it loses its autonomy. Energy is a prerequisite for independence and the satisfaction of various human needs indispensable for a fair existence: access to water, health, education, transport, employment, food conservation, and production.

It should also be noted that many means of communication, essential for the current development of peoples, make use of energy-requiring technologies. Numerous forms of information and therefore of participation in social and civil life and democracy would not be possible without energy.

For these very reasons, energy should be considered as a *common good*, as we will emphasize hereinafter, that must be guaranteed to all. *Inadequate and unequal access to energy must be, therefore, considered as an obstacle to the integral development of peoples and to a fair society.*

6. Energy, a Complex, Potentially Conflictual Factor

The management of energy at the international level is particularly complex. In fact, it first requires an interdisciplinary approach (scientific, economic, environmental, geopolitical, and social) at multiple levels, from local to global. Then, it should be remembered that energy resources coming from nature are not evenly distributed across the planet. Finally, we must not forget that there are great disparities in scientific and technological mastery, policies, production, access, and consumption of energy.

A particularly delicate aspect is the fact that energy is a strategic factor characterized by a dimension of potential conflict. In this respect, the most varied instruments of pressure and enormous economic and political interests come, indeed, into play. Moreover, being widely regarded as a need and an absolutely essential good, energy often sets communities and countries against one another in a fierce competition for the control of its sources. This explains why, in some international or multinational contexts, the need has been felt for rules to be established and intergovernmental collaborations to be started.[33]

One can well understand, therefore, that the unsound or unfair management of energy can threaten peace, "the entire ecosystem and consequently the survival of humanity."[34]

CHAPTER 2

Energy:
The Challenge of Our
Time, the Challenge for
Justice and Peace

I. Energy and Injustice

1. Unequal Distribution and Consumption on National Levels

The distribution of non-renewable primary energy sources is marked by gross territorial imbalances. Some countries are in a privileged position, as they have considerable stocks, and this is a great advantage when considering the amount of global energy currently produced and consumed deriving from non-renewable sources.

It should be pointed out, however, that the biggest holders of non-renewable energy resources are not necessarily the biggest consumers. Conversely, some countries—including many of the most civilized ones—use them in large quantities, although they do not have considerable stocks. They have acquired a privileged position thanks to their political influence, their technological level, and their economies, which have enabled them to import as much energy as deemed necessary. Moreover, import requires additional energy consumption. Inevitably, the complex relationship between countries producing and countries

21

consuming energy resources is characterized by moments of crisis and open conflict, whose consequences have mostly affected and keep affecting the poorer strata of the populations involved.

Furthermore, we must not forget the possible negative impact of fuel subsidies bestowed by the governments that can afford them, which contribute to the worldwide increase in the price of energy, even where populations or governments can hardly afford it.

The question of the energy inequality between countries should be analyzed seriously. The failure for countries to gain access to effective and adequate energy decreases or even prevents the possibilities to compete in the production of goods and the provision of services on a global scale. At the same time, it favors cyclic impoverishment, characterized by shortage of food, labor, education, and other privations.

2. Unequal Access to Technology on National Levels

The development of energy systems is strongly affected by technological inequalities. For example, there is a big gap between countries engaged in the research and development of advanced nuclear plants and those which do not even have the basic facilities to refine their own crude oil into petrol or other by-products and are sometimes obliged to export oil and import petrol.

The underlying causes of technological disparity are diverse. Many of the most exploited processes and plants in the field of energy are covered by patents of their industrial developers: their use is subject to the payment of correlative rights, which may be economically unsustainable. The most complex energy processes and plants imply thorough knowledge of advanced technologies, procedures, and methodologies, which are beyond the means of poorer countries.[1]

Disparities in access to technologies may arise in all segments of the energy sector, such as:

- extraction, refining, and storage of non-renewable primary resources: some countries and companies have modern onshore or offshore systems, while in other parts of the world, petroleum is extracted using obsolete and polluting methods that cause massive waste;

- transport: it should be remembered that the proper design and construction of networks, means, and plants for the distribution and transport of energy such as pipelines, tankers, or electrical networks affect losses of energy;
- construction, operation, and maintenance of power production plants and electrical transport and distribution networks;
- efficiency of energy production and distribution systems;
- methods and techniques of assessing the impact on health and environment both during the normal operation of the plants and in case of accidents.

3. Energy Access and Consumption on a Global and Individual Level

The energy requirement *per capita* varies considerably in the various countries and is largely related to the level of development reached.

Inequalities on a Global and Individual Level

The correlation between energy consumption and development level is not, however, such as to justify certain obvious imbalances. We are perfectly aware of the difficulty in clearly establishing what amount of energy is universally necessary to ensure the enjoyment of human rights and at least minimum standards of decent life.

Yet this does not prevent us from noting that there are significant inequalities in access to and consumption of energy. The majority of the world's population consumes only a tiny part of the global energy, while a very small percentage of them have large amounts of it. In particular, in many areas of the countries making up the G8, but also in other particularly developed areas, people consume the amount of energy sufficient for a decent standard of living several times a day.

The Dramatic Situation in Less Developed Areas

Over three billion people, basically in development countries, rely on traditional biomasses—mainly wood—for food preparation and heating. An estimated 1.2 billion people are without electricity[2] and, even where it is available, millions of people cannot afford buying it.[3] The common denominator is the fact that the lack of energy contributes to causing and spreading poverty and endangering health, especially where the performance of daily activities depends on human energy and inefficient biomass combustion alone.

Now, many of the daily activities that require energy are fundamental:

- water purification for drinking;
- lighting for reading and studying;
- heat for cooking or heating;
- transport;
- the satisfaction of certain "basic needs" such as, depending on the contexts, the use of household appliances to keep several products (e.g., medicines and vaccines) cool, and the operation of machines like simple pumps for irrigation or toilet devices.

Where these daily activities are not made possible by the lack of energy, we cannot talk about acceptable standards of living.

Energy Poverty in Developed Countries

For several decades, industrial countries have been increasingly aware that low-income families become particularly vulnerable to the relentless increase in the cost of energy. Such vulnerability

24

has been manifest especially in the wake of the oil price shocks occurring periodically since 1973, and today it affects tens of millions of people.

This condition of energy poverty is mainly due to the interaction of several factors: low-income families, homes insulated in a superficial way, inefficient and dispersive energy systems, high prices for energy supplies, sometimes due to pure speculation, and so on.

This phenomenon affects a wide range of families and individuals to varying degrees. The most exposed type of household combines low income levels with additional degrees of social vulnerability, as in the case of old people, disabled people, and single-income families.

Inequality, a Global Challenge

As we have seen, while the lack of energy can represent the dividing line between life and death for many people in poor countries, it can constitute the difference between poverty and acceptable standard of living for low-income families in developed countries.

Ultimately, energy poverty is a crucial aspect in the daily life of all peoples, including the richer ones. The increase in the cost of energy for households and the current serious international economic crisis are quickly multiplying risks.

The first judgment about a similar situation is that every strong and unjustified disparity in the distribution of energy cannot truly conform to the designs of the all-wise Creator.[4]

4. Imbalances in the Consequences of Energy Production and Consumption and of Resource Extraction

The economic, environmental, and social costs resulting from the use of common energy resources are not always fully borne by those who incur them.[5] In various contexts, it seems that the biggest energy consumers are just those who are most secure against such costs because of the geographical, technological, or economic situation. On the contrary, less developed communities, which only consume small amounts of energy, are highly vulnerable and have limited chances to face up to any environmental effects caused or in any case affected by the high energy consumption of advanced countries. Emblematic examples are:

- exploitation of non-renewable resource deposits, often irrespective of in-depth assessments of its impact on health and environment, not always prescribed by the legislation of the countries where such deposits are located;
- unequal distribution of the cost of pollution and of the exploitation of natural resources between countries producing and countries consuming resources;
- deforestation, perpetrated in a systematic way to obtain firewood, by communities that have no alternatives and thus severely damage the environment;
- construction of dams, which do provide precious "clean" hydroelectric energy for faraway cities and industrial centers, but often upset the life of local communities that depend on the river and do not even enjoy the electricity thus generated;
- extraction of most of oil, coal, and gas, for the use of the most advanced countries, which occurs in developing areas often without adequate respect for:
  - the protection of the environment surrounding the extraction sites, especially soil and water;
  - the health of local populations;
  - human rights, working conditions, and social structures of inhabitants, who may suffer as a result of certain extraction processes, especially when those who are responsible thereof resort to violence, to the criminalization of movements organized by civil society in defense of the population, or give

rise to territorial conflicts in an attempt to undermine or manipulate the existing social structures.

Added to this are the negative effects of unfair trade. On the one hand, some countries grow poorer because they are robbed of their energy resources from which they gain paltry compensation that usually only enriches elites. On the other hand, we see that players of other countries, such as big resource suppliers, derive substantial profits from this state of affairs.

II. Demand for Energy

1. Increased Needs and Demand

The curve of energy demand follows the progressive increase of the world population and the improvement of standards of living in various countries.[6] In addition to the numerous publications issued by international agencies, the United Nations Framework Convention on Climate Change (UNFCCC) held in 1992 already admitted that energy consumption would grow in all countries, but especially in developing ones.[7] Recent estimates of the United Nations (UN) indicate that by 2030 the world demand will increase by at least 45% compared to 2012.[8]

Besides the mere increase of the world population, this trend is due to several factors, including:

- improvement of the standard of living, which implies larger consumption for food preparation and conservation, lighting and air conditioning, as well as leisure;
- growing demand for mobility in a globalized world, which involves the production and use of a greater number of sea, land, and air means of transport for people and goods, especially over long distances;[9]
- mounting demand for consumer goods (vehicles, computers, phones, various household appliances) that

absorb a greater amount of energy for their production, transport, and use;

- development of communication and information technologies that account for about 3% of energy consumption and CO_2 emissions,[10] with an upward trend of this percentage due to the boom of the Internet, digital television, and mobile telephony, which require digital devices and data storage and transmission infrastructures that are increasingly powerful from the point of view of functions and performance.

2. Limits to the Satisfaction of Energy Demand

In view of the methods and technologies employed so far, the upward curve of energy production and consumption is already highlighting the existence of stringent limitations related to some fundamental factors, such as the depletion of fossil and mineral resources, and the impact on the environmental balance both at the local and global level. This suggests that the demand will not keep increasing indefinitely, especially in view of the current modes of energy production and consumption.

Environment

Communities, through their development and, in particular, through the energy systems currently used in the richest countries, are increasingly better able to influence the environment. It is in this spirit that the term *anthropocene* was coined, from Greek ἄνθρωπος and χαινός, later also adopted by the Pontifical Academy of Sciences. In the specific case of energy, a first limitation is due to the negative impact on the environment that its production and consumption currently have at the local and global level.

At the local level, the environment can be damaged by activities such as: the extraction of fossil and mineral resources that contaminate soil, water, and air; the construction of oil pipelines or dams that alter ecosystems; the installation of solar panels, in case they reduce or impoverish farmland; deforestation, which causes hydrogeological instability, landslides, and floods; the conscious, accidental, or negligent dispersion of highly polluting substances (chemicals, radioactive substances) in nature.[11]

Over the last few decades there has been a growing concern about the effects that certain human activities, including in particular those involving the use of energy resources, might have on the environment and especially on climate at a global level. Scientific research has so far emphasized rises in the concentration of carbon dioxide in the atmosphere and in the average temperature of the planet, which both coincide over time with the development of the industrial age. Although significant changes in the average temperature of the earth already occurred in the remote past, therefore in the absence of anthropic causes, some climatologists believe that the cause-and-effect relationship between the two aforesaid phenomena and human activity is most likely. This explains the great concern in the international sphere of science and politics for such a correlation and for its possible future serious effects (drying up of soils, melting of glaciers, rising of sea levels), the consequences of which would especially affect areas where climate balances are already precarious (semideserts, coastal plains, small islands), thus endangering certain populations.

It is clear, then, that we should look cautiously at practices involving massive atmospheric emissions[12] of CO_2[13] and other greenhouse gases, such as in particular: massive deforestation, excessive spreading of livestock farms that generate methane, burning of coal, oil, gas, wood, and urban waste.

Timber and especially fossil energy sources (i.e., sources whose use produces CO_2) are the resources that mainly feed current energy systems. In recent years, the hoped-for "decarbonization of economies" has not made the progress expected or considered necessary, despite the technological advancement, the development of renewable energy sources, and the adoption of measures such as the Kyoto Protocol, some European Directives, and a number of national policies in the field of energy.

Therefore, in view of environmental effects, real and dreaded, *the prospect of meeting greater demand for energy by simply increasing the same kind of consumption that has characterized the hitherto predominant model of development is likely to be unsustainable for the environment.*

Society, Economy, and International Competition for Non-renewable Energy Resources

A different limit is related to the reduction of non-renewable energy resources, especially fossil sources, whose very slow natural regeneration cycle cannot keep up with the ever-growing demand. Since these energy sources will continue, in the coming decades, to meet much of the demand for energy, markets could be affected by rarefaction and scarcity. The communities most at risk are those whose economies are primarily based on such resources.

The economies of the various countries, especially the most advanced ones, need an increasingly large amount of energy to pursue their growth.[14] Nevertheless, the demand for energy that inevitably goes hand in hand with development is gradually shifting the gravity center of consumption from the most advanced countries to emerging and developing ones. These latter require increasing amounts of energy, often with low efficiency levels that contribute to push up consumption. This also applies to countries that traditionally export energy resources, whose domestic demand is constantly rising. By way of example, the share of global oil consumed yearly by the richest and most advanced countries—whether they are members of the G8, the G20, or OECD—is progressively falling against the growing share consumed by countries with an emerging or developing economy.[15]

Therefore, a very intense demand will continue to encumber the non-renewable energy sources for the coming years. It could not only put into competition exporting countries with the importing ones but, ultimately, the strongest economies with the weakest economies, with the risk of severe penalties for the latter. In the logic of the growing international competition, those who fail to provide their economy with the sufficient amount of energy for immediate consumption and stockpiling are deemed losers. It is easy to observe that governments that act only on the basis of national security schemes, often associated with "exaggerated nationalism,"[16] are inclined to participate in this competition with determination and by all means they deem appropriate, having considered that their own economies—whereon their political strength, social stability, productivity, and military capacity depend—are at stake. Humanity is, therefore, faced with serious potential risks of political and economic tensions and conflicts for the control of non-renewable energy resources. In confirmation of this, it is pertinent to point out that many institutions have long carried out in-depth studies on the military implications arising from the competition for energy resources and from the deterioration of climatic conditions in large geographical areas, thus considering such implications likely, or even taking them for granted.

The negative phenomena associated with the control of non-renewable energy resources, and especially fossil resources, have already been seen clearly in the case of oil and natural gas. The constant rise in their price on the international markets has increased the cost of energy and that of the related activities and goods. The price of oil, in particular, is easily and frequently affected by not always predictable or controllable political factors, which cannot be sufficiently justified by the evolution of the amounts of oil available. In addition to this, financial transactions and *cartels* between the companies concerned have created a discrepancy between an efficient oil market and the one implemented in practice. All this has a negative impact on the global economy and creates serious problems and uncertainties for the future of the human family.

III. Obstacles to Energy Development

1. Centralized Systems and Distributed Systems: A Theoretical Opposition

We would now like to ponder on a theoretical opposition that has been ongoing for several years.

Some call for the extension of the energy development model (as well as the economic and industrial one) typical of developed or developing countries to the poorer ones; this is also reflected in the desire expressed in various ways by representatives of populations living in backward areas: "We do not want solutions for the underdeveloped: we want the same energy as richer countries have, and we want to consume as much."

Others, instead, tend to favor the adoption of a "new" development model, based on the distributed generation of electrical energy, deriving mainly, if not exclusively, from new renewable sources. While contributing to the multiplication of responsible producers, this would give rise, so to speak, to *energy democratization*.

This opposition of models is likely to prove fruitless and counterproductive for countries in need of energy development, if a possible future solution of the problem is expected without adopting adequate supporting polices.

It is not possible to impose in a top-down way a universal model of energy development. There are, indeed, several areas where multiple energy sources are available, where economic and social development has reached different levels. In other words, poor areas are not *tabulae rasae* on which to write a new abstract development model, which must instead result from a careful analysis of local conditions and from the proper use of the available or accessible resources.

Energy development models cannot be determined *a priori*, as they have evolved since the beginning of civilization and continue to do so, combining needs and resources as rationally as possible.

2. Electricity Still Far from Isolated and Poor Areas

In various developing areas, the demand is not met because the extension of the *traditional electric grids*, which distribute the electricity produced by big power plants, is hindered by the lack of infrastructure, technology, and financial resources. Creating or extending one of these grids to reach only a few homes or an isolated rural area is very expensive: such a project would probably be rejected due to lack of productivity. Should it ever be carried out, the grid would just as likely lack adequate maintenance and, little by little, it would be no longer able to distribute the expected energy. In both cases, those areas are unlikely to be supplied with electricity.

This means that many of the areas without electricity—frequent in less advanced countries—cannot count on or hope to be reached by traditional electric grids in the near future because it would take years of work and investment. The great number of abandoned or incomplete grids scattered around the world is evidence of these lacks.

3. Corruption and *Bad Governance*

In developing countries, the discovery of energy resources often turns into a disaster for local populations and the neighboring environment. This is especially true of oil.

Large sums of money are invested by companies, lobbies, and states to obtain concessions for the extraction of oil. Frequently, this coveted resource can be found in developing areas, characterized by: weakness of institutions, due to their shortage or their management by corrupted and/or poorly trained personnel; inadequacy of control mechanisms, due to their inability to verify or enforce compliance with the law; limited transparency; fragility of administrative procedures and democracy. The injection of large sums of money in corrupted and ill-governed structures, complicit in the failure to protect the environment and people, can only have deleterious effects. As a matter of fact, the leaders of such structures are primarily interested in the immediate income generated by oil, without worrying about the social[17] or environmental consequences resulting from the hoarding of natural resources, or to seek alternative and sustainable sources of income.

Furthermore, these structures undermined by corruption are often connected with conflicts on various scales.[18]

In the historical evidence of facts, what impairs the development of large areas of the world has not been and is not only the lack of energy and natural resources, but more often the bad use made of them by local governments.

IV. Particular Challenges

We wish to draw attention here to some particular challenges related to energy, which make its management even more complex.

1. The Charm of Being Green and the Necessary Precautions

States, cities, companies, and even individuals can aspire to be "green." Being or at least appearing "green" is a trend supported by several reasons, which require serious discernment.

There are, first of all, the reasons of those who are concerned about the sustainability of the environment and its natural resources, or about the climate.

Others are, instead, dictated by geopolitical needs, such as: reducing dependence on costly fossil resources; getting rid of energy suppliers deemed unreliable; limiting the accumulation of great wealth in the hands of certain exporters of fossil resources, belonging to organizations whose transparency can hardly be ascertained, which could also reveal links with the world of crime or terrorism.

One's desire to appear technologically advanced or attempt to offer a captivating image of oneself in advertising, commercial, or electoral contexts are frequent.

Now, some of these reasons are no doubt good and valid. Others seem to lack solidity and foresight, because they often appear to follow cultural *clichés* or opportunistic commonplaces, or even to be supported cynically by individuals who are not really concerned about the environment or human development, but only aim to achieve certain personal goals.

Because of all this, programs, projects, or slogans that flaunt "green" evolutions should be considered with caution. The development of renewable or however increasingly clean energy is important and should be supported, but we must recognize that the compatibility of power plants with the context for which they have been designed is not always adequately assessed: relevance of the technologies chosen, space consumption, impact of intermittences in the supply of energy when they are not able to function, for example in the hours with no sunshine for solar energy or no wind for wind power. Also for these reasons, in the event of investments promoted as particularly "green," there have been cases, especially in developing areas but not only, of energy power plants built without the necessary preconditions for their economically sustainable and lasting exploitation, wherefore they have been subsequently abandoned.

Finally, it is important that the improvement of the standard of living in a city or country is not achieved at the expense of other cities or countries. One cannot claim the merit of contributing to environmental sustainability or of acting positively on climate change, when the implementation of "green" measures deteriorates other people's environment or compromises their access to food and other resources.

Exportation of Pollution

In order to improve environmental standards and to reduce production costs, states and companies have outsourced not only the most polluting and energy-consuming production cycles, but also the management of too often hazardous waste, expensive to dispose of, such as scrap metal, industrial, chemical, pharmaceutical, hospital, or radioactive waste. It is clear that this behavior does not contribute to solve the environmental issue,[19] but it only transfers it, mostly to countries with less demanding regulations about the protection of the environment and of workers, whose inhabitants have little chance to defend themselves from the consequences of pollution.

Management of Biofuels

In order to reduce the consumption of fossil fuels in the transport sector, many countries have opted in recent decades for the development and production of fuels based on alcohol and oils derived from the industrial processing of agricultural products (in general, cereal, sugary, and oily crops). These biofuels are considered renewable energy sources, because their combustion simply returns to the environment the CO_2 that plants from which they derive have absorbed from the atmosphere and stored as carbon in fibers during their vegetative life.

In the field of biofuels, a quickly established international market allows operators to transfer a large part of the product from producer countries to importer countries. The earnings deriving from the production and trading of biofuels have thus become an essential component of the economy of some producer countries and of several industrial organizations, contributing to the massive development of intensive agriculture directed to this purpose.

OECD and FAO[20] estimate that, at the global level, a considerable part of such crops will continue in the future to be used for the production of biofuels, which are considered as the main opportunity to develop renewable and sustainable fuels for the transport industry as an alternative to oil.

However, there are concerns arising from the analysis of the social, environmental, and economic impact—often disregarded and sometimes negative[21]—associated with their production and use.

Among the dangers, most important are those resulting from the conversion of crops otherwise intended for food use. On the one hand, it favors farmers by allowing them to gain access to two outlets: they can sell the agricultural product to customers of both the food market and the energy one, for the transformation into fuel. On the other hand, however, there is a risk of tying up the price of a foodstuff to that of fuels, which is established on a global rather than local level, and may be subject to speculation and rapid variations. By way of example, in countries where maize is part of the base of nutrition, disastrous consequences of the increase in its price have already been observed. Various studies have attributed this price rise to its increasing use in the production of biofuels.

Another danger is, in certain rural areas, the conversion of crops mainly intended to supply the local food market into crops of plants that are inedible or anyway little used for food, with the purpose of using them to produce energy. This trend results in the gradual loss of vast plots of farmland that might be cultivated for food and livestock use, with significant repercussions on the availability of food at the local level. There are also evident financial risks: in the absence of clear and respected agreements between producers and buyers, or also owing to variations in the market of energy products, farmers may not be able to sell their crops at profitable prices. In this case, they would suffer strong damage, since products could not be placed on the food market.

Finally, a number of experts focus on the lack of a careful management—supported by adequate scientific knowledge—of the competition for water and land between crops intended for the production of biofuels and those intended for food.

2. Use of Wood as a Source of Energy

Special attention should be given to the simple and traditional energy deriving from wood.[22] As mentioned above, wood is considered a renewable source of energy, because man can manage forests in a sustainable manner. However, it should be borne in mind that wood is considered a climatically neutral and socially acceptable source of energy only if its use complies with certain conditions, including, precisely, the sustainable management of forests and its efficient use, which can be achieved by minimizing potential energy losses and emissions both inside and outside homes.

In many poor countries, firewood is still the main energy source for cooking food and heating; also in developed countries, it is used as a supplementary energy source for home heating.

In poor countries, the use of wood as a source of energy mainly relies on simple and traditional technologies like open fireplaces. In developed countries, more complex technologies have been gradually introduced: for example, the controlled combustion in closed fire systems, such as pellet stoves, which ensure, among other things, the optimal energy exploitation of residues resulting from working processes that wood undergoes for its many forms of use.

The massive use of firewood is not, however, exempt from environmental and sometimes health concerns.

Mass Energy for Basic Needs

Worldwide, nearly 2.7 billion people depend on traditional biomasses,[23] of which—according to the analyses of FAO—over 2 billion depend on energy supplied by wood for food preparation and heating, especially in developing countries and in areas where it is the only energy resource available or that families can afford.

Wood, the par-excellence traditional and decentralized bioenergy, represents one third of the global renewable energy consumption.[24] It is the predominant source for over one third of the current world population, who primarily burn it for cooking. This, in some cases, makes wood an essential component of the right to food.[25] Therefore, in certain circumstances, this right prevails over environmental considerations.

Impact of Deforestation on the Environment

Deforestation—although its annual growth has been declining since 2010—remains an alarming phenomenon. According to FAO, the uncontrolled and reckless conversion of forests into farmland, which takes place at a worrying pace,[26] is a major cause of deforestation, in addition to lucrative wood trade and urban sprawl. In this regard, two observations can be made.

The first regards those areas that, because of their climate and their abundant availability of water, are particularly suitable for cultivation. These areas, especially where they allow more than one crop a year, are ideal for the production of biofuels. This peculiarity makes tropical forests—which provide "an essential contribution to the regulation of the earth's climatic conditions [and] possess one of the richest varieties of the earth's species"[27]—particularly threatened. FAO also raises alert over the responsibility for deforestation aimed at the production of biofuels, for example in Asia[28] and in the Amazon region.[29]

The second observation concerns the relationship between forests and poorer populations, who often contribute to deforestation by practicing *slash-and-burn*[30] for their subsistence farming. Over two billion of these people—as already mentioned—use firewood as fuel for cooking, thus contributing to deforestation.

These same people often have combustion technologies characterized by very low energy efficiency, since rudimentary stoves and cookers burn a lot more wood than otherwise required. The relationship that poorer and more vulnerable people have with forests, as pointed out by John Paul II, is an "unfortunate proof of how inappropriate means can be used for good or even necessary aims. In this case the solution of an urgent problem can create another, equally serious one."[31]

The survival and balance of forests is now an environmental concern of great importance, also with reference to climatic balances. However, it should be noted that no environmental concern that pushes, for example, to preserve forests must prevail over the basic need to cook and eat, even by knocking down trees, in the absence of alternative energy sources. All efforts must therefore be directed to ensuring increasingly greater availability of these sources and wider access.

Outdoor Pollution

The question of pollution in urban areas is of a highly complex nature, both because the majority of the population lives here, with consequent problems of exposure and effects on health, and because cities themselves represent a significant source of pollution.

The contribution to urban pollution resulting from the domestic combustion of firewood, even in the form of pellets, reaches up to 60% of the particle mass concentration in the atmosphere and is largely responsible for the difference in the concentration of organic particles registered between winter and summer.[32] Since systems for domestic use in general have no fume reduction devices, the increase in their use poses a serious problem of air quality and impact on health for the coming years.

Wood combustion produces several polluting substances, many of which are classified as toxic (carbon monoxide, formaldehyde, dioxins) or as carcinogenic (polycyclic aromatic compounds and benzopyrene). In many cities of developed countries, fireplaces and wood stoves are considered the main source of ultrafine particles. 90% of wood smoke consists of powders with average size of less than one millionth of a meter (μm, microns). These are so tiny that they can be airborne for weeks and penetrate into pulmonary alveoli, becoming efficient vehicles of toxic gases, bacteria, and viruses and causing serious damage, since they go directly into the bloodstream.

Indoor Pollution

The domestic use of low-grade fuels for cooking and heating can have negative effects on indoor places and produce serious health consequences in those who live there. This is true especially for the neediest populations, who live in underdeveloped areas and in rooms without proper ventilation. Under these conditions, people are directly exposed to combustion fumes, with harmful consequences for the health, especially of women and children.

The threat to human health derives from the presence of particulate matter in smoke, which increases the incidence, duration, and seriousness of respiratory diseases when inhaled, affecting especially children, the elderly, and people with heart or lung diseases. Air pollutants also cause damage to the immune system, asthma, allergies, autoimmune diseases, psychological disorders, and toxic damage to the nervous system and the brain.

In extreme cases in which wood is not available, other even more harmful fuels, such as dung, plastics, or garbage, are used for cooking. UN estimates that indoor pollution kills about two million people every year.[33]

3. Sustainability of Cities

Growing Cities with Growing Needs

The question of the sustainable satisfaction of energy requirements stands in close relation to the growing tendency to urbanization of the world population. Urban areas account for about two thirds of the total consumption of primary energy sources.[34] Now, current estimates envisage not only the increase of the world population—with the consequent increase of the demand for energy—but also the gradual expansion of cities. The number of megalopolises inhabited by millions of people is expected to grow in the coming decades. According to UN estimates, two thirds of humanity will live in towns and cities within two generations, compared to about half today.[35] This trend, if not properly governed and managed, is likely to generate serious problems for the sustainability of cities and the balance of their constituting systems and structures.

The challenge of providing cities with food, water, and energy, ensuring draining of waste water and refuse, and of managing transport-related issues is and will remain difficult in advanced countries and extremely arduous in developing ones.

(Un)Sustainable Cities

The sustainability problems of cities mainly stem from the fact that they are not independent from the point of view of food, nor are they able to produce all the energy they need. Moreover, the expansion of urban settlements often occurs to the detriment of cultivated or cultivable areas, thus favoring food insecurity and land degradation.

Since cities are not autonomous, they are particularly vulnerable to external factors that can affect supplies and stocks. Should the supply routes or the energy pipelines of a city with millions of inhabitants be stopped suddenly, episodes of dramatic chaos would occur in a few days.

In large cities, given the concentration of emissions, serious pollution problems are also likely to occur,[36] requiring solution since harmful to the health and the environment. UN-HABITAT, for example, estimates that "greenhouse gas emissions spewed out by cities account for up to 70% of the world's pollution—much of it coming from our fossil fuel consumption for electricity, transport, energy use in commercial and residential buildings, industrial production and waste."[37]

The production, transport, and use of energy in large urban centers must therefore be carefully considered when planning, designing, managing, and controlling the related activities. Cities, in particular, are the places where it is necessary and possible to promote the environmental compatibility and energy efficiency of systems and equipment at all levels and with the utmost commitment.

Poor Neighborhoods Bound to Fail?

The sustainability problems that affect large urban settlements are amplified considerably in the most disadvantaged parts of cities and, in particular, of cities in underdeveloped countries.

Today about one third of the urban population lives in very poor neighborhoods, also known as slums or *bidonville* or *asentamiento humano* or *favela*. These are often suburban districts consisting of rudimentary hovel agglomerates or more rarely of run-down buildings, which were set up in a short time, in a succession of sudden waves of people fleeing drought, rural poverty, or conflicts. The establishing mechanism of these neighborhoods makes any urban planning very difficult—even if not impossible, provided technical capabilities and economic resources are available.

In many cases, these neighborhoods, which do not offer job opportunities and have seriously inadequate health and education systems, can hardly be provided with services such as sewer systems, water, and electricity, and their possible improvement would take a long time and much investment. Here, living conditions are sometimes so degraded as not to allow the promotion of the fundamental rights of the human person.

A challenge that world leaders are called on to solve is precisely to remedy the situation in slums and to provide their inhabitants with essential services, including energy. An even greater challenge is to succeed—in a spirit of prevention—in improving the desperate living conditions that force millions of people to crowd in these slums, sometimes situated in areas that are particularly dangerous for seismic hazards, flooding, or other. The development of a cautious policy in this sense would avoid having to manage such dramatic scenarios in the future.

4. Energy and Food Security

Scarcity of Food or Energy: Similar Situations

The analyses carried out in the international arena show that, globally, the number of people suffering from food shortage is approximately equal to the number of people suffering from energy shortage. It also seems that the people in question live in the same areas.[38]

In a 2010 Declaration, the General Assembly of the United States noted that "one and a half billion people are without electricity and that, even when energy services are available, millions of poor people are unable to pay for them."[39] For its part, FAO points out that four fifths of the people without electricity live in rural areas of developing countries.[40]

FAO also notes that nearly two billion people suffer from one or more micronutrient deficiencies and that, in 2011–2013, 842 million people were unable to meet their dietary energy requirements, the vast majority of which lived in developing countries.[41]

According to the sources cited above, there are clear connections between the scarcity of food and of energy in poorer areas. Approximately 1 person in 3 or 4 is the victim of both these shortages. Therefore, in the challenge for development, the issues of food and energy shortages need to be addressed jointly.

The Link between Food and Energy

The agro-food sector depends in an essential way on the availability of energy. Energy is intensively used in agriculture and animal husbandry to construct buildings and infrastructure, to operate the mechanical means used for working and fertilizing the land, to pump water necessary for irrigation, and for the functioning of livestock installations. In the chemical industry related to agriculture, energy is used for the production of fertilizers, pesticides, and animal feed. In the agro-food industry, it is necessary to processing plants. Finally, energy is indispensable in the phases of storage, transport, and distribution of the foodstuffs produced, as well as for their preparation before consumption.

The production of food occupies, therefore, a prominent position in global energy consumption[42] and still depends largely on fossil fuels, especially oil, coal, and methane. This is a delicate challenge, if one considers the relentless rise in the cost of these raw materials and the concurrent need to reduce emissions of greenhouse gases.

Humanity has a growing need for food and energy. According to UN estimates, the world population will reach 9.1 billion by 2050. To meet the expected demand for food, FAO believes that agricultural production will have to increase by 70% in 40 years. Only 10% of the increase in food production is expected to be resulting from an expansion of arable land: the remaining 90% will necessarily originate from the intensification of crops.[43] With regard to energy, the hoped-for intensification cannot be achieved by mainly aiming at the increased consumption of the relatively inexpensive fossil energy that contributed significantly to feed the world in the past decades, but at higher energy efficiency[44] and at the procurement of new energy sources. The improvement of energy efficiency and energy savings in the production and management of food must take into account, among other things, the shocking fact that about one third of the food for human consumption in the world is wasted,[45] even because "consumerism has induced us to be accustomed to excess and to the daily waste of food."[46]

Furthermore, the agriculture of the future will have to be increasingly able to reduce its impact on ecosystems at a global level and the impact of its emissions. The challenge, in short, demands greater production and lower pollution and consumption at the same time.

It is pertinent to remember here what has already been said about crops not intended for food, but for the production of biofuels or, anyway, of energy products, such as biogas. In certain contexts, this creates or enhances a competition between food production and energy production, with a rise in the prices of agricultural products induced by the high market prices of energy products.[47]

Finally, it should be noted that the production of certain foods is highly energy-consuming and therefore, reasonably "modest behavior and consumption"[48] is indispensable, especially in advanced countries. One such example is beef, which absorbs huge energy resources for the production of feed, breeding, slaughtering, transport, and storage.

The competition in the use of soils has already had the effect of a huge increase in the demand for land. This is testified by the phenomenon of *land grabbing*, which is the acquisition of large arable plots of land, especially in less developed countries, by investors who act on behalf of governments or agro-food companies. Given the high market price of energy products, driven upward by the continuous increase in the price of oil, market mechanisms tend to boost the demand for agricultural products to be processed for energy uses, favoring the use of the land for such purposes and thus subtracting it to food consumption. This "monopolization of cultivable areas"[49] is a trend closely related to market malfunctioning, which is likely to have a negative impact on food security also in this case. This trend is favored in many developed countries by the adoption of regulations that promote and encourage the use of agricultural products for energy purposes.

5. Nuclear Energy

With reference to justice and peace, the complex issue of nuclear energy is crucial. Provided that nuclear disarmament and the complete deviation of nuclear material and funding must advance from military purposes to peaceful activities, the question of the so-called *civil* or *peaceful nuclear power*[50] holds particular relevance. In fact, our age seems to be characterized by:

- international negotiations focusing on the access to the production of nuclear energy by further states;[51]
- the search for energy sources that can meet a growing demand consistent with sustainable development;
- concerns about security due to the risks associated with the use of nuclear energy—dreaded or occurred—for both individuals, entire communities, and the environment.

With reference to the issue of peaceful nuclear power, we should first say that it ought to be approached without prejudices or ideological schemes, always keeping the human person and his integral development as a reference point in discussions. Another central aspect of civil nuclear power is that of security, which must be continually pursued and improved at various levels (widespread adoption of stringent safety standards, training of technical personnel, testing of facilities, promotion of a safety culture in the society in general) and requires a solid framework (international agreements, scientific cooperation and solidarity, transparency, etc.) at the same time.[52] In connection with such evaluation and safety needs, the question of research that could lead to further positive developments for civil nuclear power, such as the evolution toward safer and more effective reactors, is also important.

Talking about civil nuclear power, the difference between *nuclear technology* and *nuclear energy* should be borne in mind whenever possible and relevant. It is an important distinction, not frequently made by those who "totally" oppose the nuclear sector, at all costs, and thus omit and neglect the positive aspects emerging from the study of the atom.

With regard to technology, it is worth mentioning the beneficial applications in the medical field (in diagnostic radiology and nuclear medicine), in agriculture (in the fight against diseases and infestations, in the improvement of soil fertility) and in the environmental sphere (in the fight against soil erosion and land degradation, in the study of water resources, pollution, or the impact of ocean acidification).[53] As regards the nuclear production of electrical energy for civil uses, it is fundamental to reflect with particular caution and discernment, adopting at least two important points of view: environmental and health, also at the same time technical and economic.

The first urges us to consider the well-known benefits of nuclear energy, such as the almost total absence of greenhouse gas emissions and the reduced amount of fuel used. It also pushes us to evaluate and carefully monitor the entire energy production cycle and in particular the operation of power plants, under both *normal* conditions (procurement of raw materials, water consumption, management of solid or liquid residues, more or less polluting or radioactive, etc.) and *exceptional* conditions (faults, other emergency situations, for example, related to particularly serious or intense events).

The second point of view requires reflecting not in an abstract way, but by contextualizing the possible use of nuclear energy or its future development, with respect to the estimates of energy requirements divided by geographical areas and choices about which energy sources are most appropriate, in an analysis logic based on "costs—benefits—risks—alternatives."

6. Water and Energy

Water should be considered and safeguarded as a universal good, indispensable for life, for the integral development of peoples and for peace. In particular, it is generally recognized that the lack of drinking water is one of the main factors of underdevelopment.[54] Just as for the availability of food, the availability of water—and especially drinking water—is closely related to the availability of energy.[55]

In countries that have abundant resources of surface freshwater or groundwater, energy is necessary for the construction and operation of hydraulic intake and purification works, as well as aqueducts and distribution systems. Where freshwater resources are poor or lacking, purification requires huge amounts of energy for the desalination of seawater or brackish groundwater. This is well known by the leaders of the world's arid regions, who resort or plan to resort to desalination to obtain drinking water.

The majority of people without drinking water live in rural areas of developing countries. In these areas, greater investment in infrastructure and energy for water purification is essential.[56] Their high cost has so far prevented a significant improvement of the situation.

The link between water availability and energy availability is also effective vice-versa to what has been illustrated so far. The production of energy often requires water and some evaporation processes pollute it or consume it, making it unsuitable or insufficient for other uses. Among these processes are:

- the cooling of thermoelectric and nuclear power plants, with consequent evaporation, albeit to a minor extent;
- the construction of large dams, whose impact on the course of rivers and on the surrounding areas can decrease the amount of water available locally or adversely alter the ecosystems;
- the extraction and refining of oil, which generate polluted water that is not always duly purified;
- crops planned for the production of biofuels, which raise significant concerns about the pressure on aquatic systems.[57]

7. The Inadequate International Energy Governance

The management of energy, marked by conflicts and injustices, testifies to the inadequacy of the existing international institutions, since they do not seem to be able to create the necessary conditions in this sector for the global common good.

This can be verified, in particular, with reference to "energy externalities," which are not limited to the state or national sphere. A radioactive leak, a rupture of an oil well in the sea, or even CO_2 emissions are not limited locally, but have a regional and sometimes global impact, which lays bare the ineffectiveness of the current governance.

In fact, there is no supranational authority in charge of regulating the behavior of transnational players, who can hardly be monitored at the national and regional level. This is the case of some oligopolistic multinationals operating in the sector of energy, not always in an exemplar manner. Weak or inexistent governance is undeniably an incentive for the so-called *free riders*, who appropriate the benefits while others pay the costs.

The Inadequacy of Institutions

It is appropriate to stress the inadequacy of the international institutions with respect to energy. The International Energy Agency is made up of only twenty-eight OECD countries: therefore, it does not include the majority of world states, among which are some of the major energy consumers in the world and, in any case, it is not a governance institution. Even the *Energy Charter Treaty*, an intergovernmental treaty that requires signatories to apply impartial market rules to energy products and services, is not fully represented worldwide. Moreover, several states ranking among the major producers and consumers of fossil energy are not full members of this treaty.

The International Renewable Energy Agency, established in 2009, does enjoy greater representation, but cannot be considered as a governance structure for energy, since its role is limited to the simple promotion of renewable energy alone, with no possibility of effective interstate coordination.

Finally, the trade agreements hoped for by the World Trade Organization apply to energy in a very marginal way, since it is considered in many cases as an exhaustible natural resource, exempt, therefore, from legislation.

The Inadequacy of the Market "Alone"

Mainly because of its negative environmental externalities, the current market, in its deregulated state, is not a useful governing mechanism, since it is unable to assess environmental costs. It is estimated, for example, that the most polluting fossil sources should be subject to high taxation, to compensate for their negative externalities. Those who promote "the absolute autonomy of markets"[58] should be reminded that the free market has operating difficulties,[59] also due to the lack of information about the sector, since it is technically difficult to be obtained—for example, with regard to the ownership of a gas reserve—and is often considered confidential. In fact, governments consider their own natural resources strategic and rarely disclose information about them. Big companies that procure energy resources act likewise toward their suppliers. The many initiatives promoted by civil society in favor of greater surveillance, transparency, and traceability in this economic sector are evidence of the imbalances created and maintained by the free market. In addition to this, the *energy-related timeframe* is usually long—as are its effects on the environment and the amortization of investment—and markets are unable to take due account of it because of their intrinsic volatility.

V. An Economic Model Called into Question

1. Irresponsible Profit Seeking

The current dominant economic model can be described as a tension toward continuous growth, which must be accessed by more and more people, with the prospect of unlimited consumption. This model, based on and associated with the energy parameters of the more developed countries, is unsustainable. We need, therefore, to revise the logic of economies and markets, now marked by utilitarian and consumerist criteria.

The Church acknowledges the legitimate role of profit as an indication of the good performance of companies and economies in general: from the presence of profit, it can be inferred that productive factors have been properly employed and corresponding human needs have been duly satisfied. However, profitability is not the only indication of a positive trend: it is possible for the financial accounts to be in order, and yet for the people to be humiliated, their dignity offended, and the ecosystem compromised. Besides being morally inadmissible, this will have negative repercussions also on economic efficiency.[60]

The environment is adversely affected also by the management of business enterprises conceived in line with the canons of the current unregulated financial capitalism, according to which everything must be subject to the speculative requirements of short-term profit, which only takes into account the interest of shareholders and disregards all the other subjects, not worrying about the natural environment[61] and social degradation. If and when it does, it is mostly due to pragmatic opportunism, since the excessive deterioration of the environment and communities risks compromising profit, wherefore it should be avoided as much as necessary to safeguard earnings.

2. Unsustainable Life

"In the developed countries there is sometimes an excessive promotion of purely utilitarian values, with an appeal to the appetites and inclinations towards immediate gratification,"[62] pointed out John Paul II. His successor, Benedict XVI, reaffirmed that absolutized consumerism is deceptively presented as the means to achieve happiness, as the good of the person. The accumulation of consumer goods is consequently encouraged by entities driven by greed for profit and promoted by mass media as a life model.[63]

The unbridled search for new short life cycle products that devour energy and soon become obsolete appears to be never-ending. Moreover, these products are designed to encourage dependence and a sense of need. All this contributes to maximizing profits and maintaining an unsustainable energy paradigm, which allows some people to use plenty of energy, while others lack the minimum needed for a decent life, as well as the economic means to gain access to sufficient energy.[64]

For ethical reasons, the options of continuing to reserve the lifestyles of consumer societies for a small elite or of boasting them as an example of ideal progress for all are therefore unacceptable.

3. The Limits of Poorly Formulated Approaches

The model that aims to universally replicate and promote the one followed by the most developed countries should be called into question. This model consists in providing everybody with enough energy to be consumed in the same amount and for the same uses (including and especially the unnecessary ones!) today emblematic of "modern" countries, which are based on approximately 80% of the fossil resources available. This is not realistic, it is not sustainable for either the societies or the environment, and may not be allowed in a sustainable manner by the existing reserves. On the other hand, as we have already seen, energy systems are constantly changing, and their mixes, adoptable in various places, depend on multiple criteria. Therefore, there is no point in talking about a "modern" universal energy model.

VI. Threats to Peace

In recent years, various crises—including repeated acts of piracy, coups d'état, and conflict with regional impact—have been triggered by energy questions or, however, issues somehow related to energy, especially in areas of extraction or transit. Some of the geopolitically hottest areas are precisely those where antagonist interests aim to oil, gas, and water. On the basis of the news in recent years, one can mention various regions of Africa or the Caucasus, in addition to transit areas frequently subjected to tensions or acts of piracy, such as some sea routes or regions crossed by gas or oil pipelines, or where they are planned to be built.

Regarding the energy infrastructure often targeted by several acts of terrorism, a delegation from the Holy See insisted in one of its interventions that steps be taken toward its security.[65]

There are also some energy conflicts, often ignored by geopolitical reflections on an international scale. These are hotbeds of despair and revolt, which arise within a single state, where fossil resource extraction projects supported by governments collide with the lifestyle of local people in close contact with the environment, as it happens in several parts of the African continent or the American one. Moreover, we should not ignore the problems related to water reserves, which governments or private operators assign to the production of hydroelectric power. The construction of dams brings about tensions when the rivers in question flow through several states. These result both from the rivalry between the various states that fail to share water in solidarity, and from the diverging interests between the energy supply of urban or industrial centers on the one hand, and the protection of land and sources of water traditionally used by some communities on the other hand.

It is really regrettable that ambitions and particular interests lead to forms of violence in relation to common goods, to resources necessary for a decent life.

More than twenty years ago, Saint John Paul II declared that the world peace was threatened by the lack of respect for nature and the plundering of its resources.[66] Since then, despite greater awareness of such questions, the situation has not improved much. On the contrary, the race on hoarding is still going on and is likely to trigger serious conflicts among peoples that "are often fought on the soil of those same countries [rich in deposits], with a heavy toll of death, destruction and further decay."[67] The consequences of the conflicts arising from the competition—the appropriation of resources by the "winner," as well as the "privations, the threat of famine and epidemics, and the nightmare of further victims and still greater suffering"[68]—penalize especially the more vulnerable native populations.

This is sadly emblematic of African oil-producing regions, which have become the scene of prolonged local conflicts, of low intensity but with international implications, for the control of resources.

We are faced with a vicious circle: the race for resources generates conflicts, and conflicts, in turn, squander or make resources unusable,[69] so that their shortage worsens and the fight for supply becomes fiercer.

In short, *considering the current trends in the field of energy, we increasingly risk being ensnared in an unstable situation, with various hotbeds of conflicts for the control of energy.* Such a situation is more and more difficult to control and might deteriorate with terrible consequences.

CHAPTER 3

Energy, an Instrument for Real Development, Justice, and Peace

I. Need for a New Energy Paradigm

The inadequacy of non-consensual, pragmatic or opportunistic short-term solutions to complex social and ethical problems has been shown all too clearly by the recent global financial crisis,[1] and this is also true about the energy question.

Humanity must free itself from the frantic pursuit of profit for profit's sake and renounce welfare dependence and pressures, whether ideological, political, economic, or military. It should also give up opportunistic attitudes, such as the supply of as much energy as needed to avoid conflicts or revolts, or to allow the merely economic development of poor areas with the only purpose of obtaining more consumers and customers; or the respect for the environment, as much as needed not to incur fines, to appear "green," not to jeopardize future profits. In particular, the social responsibility of business enterprises and the political decisions must free themselves from opportunism and cynicism, and be devoted with sincerity and responsibility to the common good. Every economic decision is also an ethical decision.[2]

57

A new paradigm about the way to produce, consume, and distribute energy is required for the development challenge and the sustainability of creation. This new paradigm must provide us all with new behavioral patterns based on justice, responsibility, altruism, subsidiarity, and the conception of the integral development of peoples with a view to the common good. These are the values that will enable humanity to successfully solve the energy question.

This new paradigm must also generate the sufficient impetus to establish sound forms of international cooperation and finance and economy administration, and make them work, to encourage and share research, to pursue laborious sustainable development, to overcome imbalances between the few exceedingly rich and the unnumbered poor, in the light of social justice and the related global common good.[3]

1. Energy, a Common Good with a Universal Destination

"The original source of all that is good is the very act of God, who created both the earth and man, and who gave the earth to man so that he might have dominion over it by his work and enjoy its fruits. God gave the earth to the whole human race for the sustenance of all its members, without excluding or favoring anyone. This is the foundation of the universal destination of the earth's goods. The earth, by reason of its fruitfulness and its capacity to satisfy human needs, is God's first gift for the sustenance of human life."[4] This reflection of John Paul II echoes that of Leo XIII, who, by the end of 1800, wrote that "nature [...] owes to man a storehouse that shall never fail, the daily supply of his daily wants. And this he finds only in the inexhaustible fertility of the earth."[5]

Universal Destination and Its Implications

Hence, the task of making sure that "under the leadership of justice and in the company of charity, created goods should be in abundance for all in like manner. Whatever the forms of property may be, as adapted to the legitimate institutions of peoples, according to diverse and changeable circumstances, attention must be always paid to this universal destination of earthly goods. In using them, therefore, man should regard the external things that he legitimately possesses not only as his own but also as common in the sense that they should be able to benefit not only him but also others."[6]

The Social Doctrine of the Church recognizes that "in keeping with the social nature of man, the good of each individual is necessarily related to the common good"[7] and, by "common good,"[8] it means "the sum of those conditions of life which allow social groups and their individual members relatively thorough and ready access to their own fulfillment."[9]

Access to energy—and to the various energy sources or resources, as well as to all the other natural resources—is one of the conditions for today's realization of the common good. Energy resources are and remain constitutively intended for a universal purpose.[10] They must be husbanded as such, "not only because humanity as a whole today may benefit, but also the generations to come."[11] This leads us to reflect on the necessary intergenerational solidarity also regarding the activities related to energy and to the distribution of resources.

Sustainability

This principle of universal destination, therefore, incorporates and transcends that of sustainability. In this regard, the gradual growth of environmental awareness has led in recent decades to the development and the progressive establishment of the *concept of sustainability*, which must not be absolutized to the point of leading to a partial view. The environmental component is, indeed, certainly essential, but it is not the only one to be considered. The *concept of sustainable development* of energy systems actually implies several components, such as:

- *economic* sustainability, understood as the ability to meet needs in view of sustainable costs by individuals and the community as a whole;
- *environmental* sustainability, understood as the ability of systems to use the energy sources available, limiting the impact on the environment to an acceptable extent;
- *social* sustainability, understood as the ability to ensure human well-being and to meet needs, without imposing constrictions of biological or ethical-moral nature or unnecessarily upsetting the organization of communities or affecting their social rights.

Models, technologies, and projects for the development of energy systems, energy production, and processing cycles can be considered truly sustainable only when they satisfy reasonably and in a balanced way the various conditions of sustainability, which, taken as a whole, constitute a concept of "ethical-moral sustainability." The degree of sustainability—environmental, social, economic—of energy sources, as well as of the methods to produce, manage, and consume it, is an important indicator of how to carry out the task entrusted to us by God as stewards of creation.

2. Searching, Promoting, and Providing Energy to Everyone in Compliance with Unavoidable Conditions

As a consequence of the above, we may agree that access to energy must be guaranteed to all in compliance with certain conditions.

Technical Conditions

We assert that energy must be: *reliable,* that is technically safe and properly functioning; with the *least health and environmental impact possible* throughout the entire process from production to consumption; *suitable for the intended uses,* in terms of type of energy and power;

with *maximum efficiency*; with *adequate access*, that is, available in suitable quantities and modes for all uses that make for an acceptable standard of living.

Socio-Economic Conditions

We then affirm that this type of energy must be: *manageable in the long term*, in the sense that the various communities—depending on their level of development—must be able to provide for the management, maintenance, and repair of power plants as far as possible; sold at an *affordable price*, in case an energy service is provided; *respectful of human societies*, in the sense that it must not upset their possible traditional organization or create unnecessary dependence on networks, procedures, or bureaucracy. Energy must be *fair* and *equitable*: its management and that of the investment earmarked for it should primarily solve the shortages of the most vulnerable and poorest populations and, only subsequently, ensure greater consumption for those who already have plenty of energy.

Cultural and Political Conditions

Energy should be *supported by appropriate education and awareness*, to valorize it, limit its waste, and encourage its rational use. It must be *administered with a view to the common good*, in *solidarity* and aiming at the protection of future generations. Consequently, it cannot fall prey to speculation or conflicts, nor can it be an instrument of pressure or a means of seeking profit for profit's sake.

In the various contexts, energy must be managed in a *democratic* and *responsible* way as far as possible, with the due technical-legal control and the *coordination by the competent authorities*: in other words, the energy necessary for the various communities should be obtained through energy mixes, which also allow the participation of responsible and increasingly autonomous citizens-players, alongside passive citizens-customers, with whom large oligopolistic groups tend to interact.

3. Conditional Support to the Initiatives of the United Nations

A number of initiatives aiming at ensuring access to energy for all sprouted up around the year 2012, declared by the UN *International Year of Sustainable Energy for All*.[12] The Pontifical Council for Justice and Peace encourages such initiatives, on condition that they favor development with a view to the common good. It is, therefore, desirable that the parties concerned are committed to supplying functional energy on the conditions listed above, thus contributing to the necessary change of the energy paradigm.

II. Governance and Responsibility

According to the Social Doctrine of the Church, all the institutions must have the ultimate aim[13] of serving and promoting human dignity, and the development[14] of each person and of the whole person.[15] In short, it can be said that the promotion of the common good is the first "duty of civil authority."[16] In order to deal with the energy issue, this authority must absolutely make use of all the capabilities and means necessary for the coordinated and solidarity-based protection of this common good in its "present day conditions of implementation." This process requires harmonious and effective governance, able to manage the many disciplines involved, the various relevant levels of analysis and action, the particular challenges of every continent and every country. Bearing in mind the diverse contexts, valid and effective solutions designed for each of them, even if based on the same principles, will actually be required.

The fundamental principles of this governance are the principle of justice and that of subsidiarity, which will be analyzed in depth hereinafter. The ultimate goal of this governance must be the universal destination of goods. Specifically, this means that it must:

- allow humanity to progress in the interconnected challenge of energy-water-food-land;
- ensure that everybody has access to energy, so as to fulfill the conditions listed above as much as possible;
- set up some form of management of energy economy and finance;[17]
- foster sustainable behavior by private and public bodies, and by civil society in general.

1. Public Policies for Energy at the National Level

With respect to the objective of energy resources equitably accessible and available to all the peoples, especially the poor ones, the policies to be promoted must be courageous, decisive, and farsighted—especially since it is well known that their effect on the environment at the global level, hopefully and presumably positive, will be felt only after a long time. Policies, then, must not be influenced by particularistic interests or launched opportunistically to achieve electoral success. The world of politics must act in concert with that of science and research, in a responsible manner and with the support of civic virtues, now too little recognized and valorized by the ruling elites, forgoing immediate economic interests or party uses, which end up humiliating human dignity. *Positive law* must be based on the principles of *natural moral law*, in order to ensure respect for the dignity and the value of the human person,[18] which can be affected if access to "modern" and sustainable energy is not promoted and guaranteed to all. Therefore, adequate legislation and structures at the service of the common good are required.

2. Policies at the International Level

The international community has an urgent duty to find institutional means of solving the energy question and regulating the activities related to it, involving poor countries in the process, in order to plan together for the future. To achieve the objectives listed below, it is incumbent on all "international leaders to act jointly and to show a readiness to work in good faith."[19] In particular, the work of the international community should be supplemented by the simultaneous contribution of individual states and civil society, as well as of the various NGOs—Non-Governmental Organizations.

Necessary International Governance

In the face of energy challenges that involve the entire world and with the aim of promoting the "global common good," the human family must adopt proportionate means.[20] The Holy See has reiterated that a "shared and co-responsible management of [...] research and safety and security of energy and water supplies and of the environmental protection of the planet call for one or more international authorities with true and effective powers."[21]

Indeed, "the time has come to conceive of institutions with universal competence, now that vital goods shared by the entire human family are at stake, goods which individual States cannot promote and protect by themselves."[22] Consequently, a good management of the environment and of sustainable energy requires the international community to adopt a "true world political authority"[23] at the service of peoples, which, according to the teaching of Pius XII,[24] must be based on subsidiarity, as called for in the prophetic encyclical *Pacem in terris* of Saint John XXIII.

The Socio-Economic Objectives of the International Governance for Energy

In *Caritas in veritate*, Benedict XVI points out some of the responsibilities of individual governments and the international community, stating that the latter has an "urgent duty to find institutional means"[25] to best perform its duties.

One of the most important of such duties is to effectively oppose ways to use the environment that turn out to be harmful, in order not to leave creation depleted of its resources to future generations. Furthermore, the international community is called on to regulate the exploitation of non-renewable resources; to demand transparency of economic and social costs (externalities) arising from the use of common environmental resources, ensuring that they are fully borne by those who benefit from them and not by other peoples or future generations; to work for the necessary worldwide redistribution of energy, so that everybody can have access to it.

In particular, the international community must guide reflection for a shared, global energy strategy, able to meet every legitimate demand in the short, medium, and long term. A global strategy is also necessary to establish and pursue possible objectives regarding climate change: the adaptation to it, especially for the most vulnerable populations or parts of them; its mitigation, provided it is effective and not too expensive in social terms.

Another duty of the international community is to promote both the compliance with existing laws and the development of legislation in national systems, aimed at ensuring that everybody has access to "modern" and sustainable energy. Also in this respect, it should be noted that "the fight against corruption requires that people work together to increase transparency in economic and financial transactions and to enact within different countries uniform legislation in this area."[26]

The international community must also promote solidarity with the poorest regions and the most vulnerable populations. Patents, the diffusion of technology and knowhow and scientific cooperation must be managed to this purpose. For more effective cooperation at multiple levels—from global to local—good practices must be inventoried and promoted.

We should also include in this context the orientation of economy by the international community, in order to: decisively revive the economies affected by financial crises; promote the responsible and sustainable use of natural resources and hinder their abuse; avoid destabilizing speculation; devise *ad hoc* mechanisms to convince states and economies that apparently have more to lose than to gain from the adoption of sustainable energy policies; monitor the market of the energy sector, its many players and in particular its lobbies—especially those of finance and of non-renewable energy—and the big oligopolistic companies, ensuring that they comply with the laws, promoting transparency and systematizing monitoring procedures. This governance must administer funds for energy-related development harmoniously and globally, paying particular attention to:

- encouraging and correctly applying the necessary investments to strengthen less developed areas;
- monitoring the use of funds;
- identifying and hindering unjustified subsidies and excessive protectionist measures;
- developing innovative financing mechanisms.

The Geopolitical Objectives of the International Governance for Energy

Working with and through the various international and national authorities, and in general with all those who are responsible for peace keeping, the hoped-for governance has the duty of handling conflicts related to energy and natural resources. The parties concerned are also required to ensure a high level of vigilance to prevent the emergence of crises, and a strong commitment to deter or, if necessary, intervene to cut them off. This calls for the monitoring of particularistic interests and behavior based on the exasperation of the "reason of state" and national security.

Among the prevention activities to be promoted and encouraged are the peaceful resolution of conflicts and the search for consensual and collaborative solutions, where fierce competition for the access to fossil deposits is in progress or foreseeable.

Finally, it is striking that Benedict XVI has referred to the issue of nuclear weapons several times in recent years. In one of his *Messages for the World Day of Peace* (2006), he poses the question: "[…] what can be said, too, about those governments which count on nuclear arms as a means of ensuring the security of their countries? Along with countless persons of good will, one can state that this point of view is not only baneful but also completely fallacious."[27] In his *Message* the following year, he dwells upon the same subject with these words: "[…] disturbing issue is the desire recently shown by some States to acquire nuclear weapons. This has heightened even more the widespread climate of uncertainty and fear of a possible atomic catastrophe."[28]

In conclusion, "the commitment to encourage nonproliferation of nuclear arms, to promote a progressive and agreed upon nuclear disarmament […] is always more present and urgent."[29]

3. The Responsibility of the State

In the light of the above, "the need for joint action on the international level does not lessen the responsibility of each individual State."[30] On the contrary, each individual state has the task to "provide for the defense and preservation of common goods such as the natural and human environments, which cannot be safeguarded simply by market forces."[31]

It is up to governments to "protect such fundamental goods"[32] as energy resources and to guarantee access to "modern" and sustainable energy to all. It is their duty to do so, especially through adequate social, legal, and economic structures, and through the enforcement of international decisions.

It is also up to them to guide economic players toward the adoption of sustainable behavior for the environment and societies, when they set the rules for public-private cooperation, and launch special public policies for the management of concessions in the extraction of resources or in the distribution of electricity, as well as for the socially and environmentally responsible performance of business activities.

With regard to citizens, states must not shirk their responsibility to provide education that fosters responsible behavior.

Today, governments must, above all, resist particularistic pressures and ensure the application of monitoring and transparency measures by all the operators of the energy sector, especially energy suppliers and extractive industries. The latter can contribute to sustainable development only when they respect the environment, when their projects are well implemented and protect the rights of the people involved, and when the benefits they generate are well used.[33] Companies of the energy sector must not be able to reap particular advantages in contexts of institutionally weak states, where they could easily contribute to the deterioration of the environment and of living conditions, and to the scourge of corruption.

Moreover, administrations, along with citizens and their organizations, are required to assess the appropriateness of certain energy solutions, in the face of the dilemma of reconciling the rights of individuals or, in any case, of the populations present in a given territory, with the interests of the common good and the development of the country. In cases where the adoption of certain solutions to produce energy harms populations forced to move away and weakens their socioeconomic structures, these will have to be properly indemnified and aided toward living a decent and safe life, enjoying the benefits of the development introduced to the advantage of the whole country.

In the end, states, along with civil society, are responsible for guarding the environment and implementing human rights in their territory and the well-being of their inhabitants, as well as for promoting equitable and sustainable economic growth.

4. Civil Society

The question of energy management does not only regard a few: technicians, politicians, or administrators. It is and must be the concern of every person and the whole of civil society. The latter relies, in particular, on the help of the political community to achieve its goals. However, this does not mean that civil society can be systematically replaced in its primary responsibility. The political community serves the aims of civil society and is entrusted by it with the task of promoting all the interventions and setting up all the institutions that are indispensable to the attainment of the common good.[34] The political authority succeeds in carrying out its task if it exploits the contribution of civil society about energy questions and advocates for it to organize itself, enabling it for example: to gain access to information about energy; to have adequate structures for the protection and assertion of its rights, in order to ensure effective participation in the management of the common good; to be trained in and to become aware of the important issues related to energy and environment. Civil society maintains the ultimate responsibility, wherefore it must get mobilized to make the political community carry out its task when it proves unable to do so.

III. Principles for Energy Management

1. Point of Reference: The Human Person

The Social Doctrine of the Church is chiefly concerned about the safeguard of the dignity of every single person, created in the image and likeness of God. "The beginning, the subject and the goal of all social institutions is and must be the human person."[35] "Among the numerous and complex variables of a political and economic nature, the essential point of reference remains, in fact, the human person, with his dignity and his fundamental rights."[36] The focal point to be always borne in mind is the centrality of man, as the subject and goal of all actions. Therefore, it is necessary to foster the dignity of every person, including those yet to be born. In this perspective, access to energy is not a goal in se, but it must be directed to the good of humanity and its development. It is an interdisciplinary task, which needs the contribution of different scientific and human competences. In order for this service to man to be possible, suitable public spaces must be created for proper interdisciplinary confrontation. In these spaces, the Church, expert in humanity, has a right of presence and a duty at the same time: it must pose, as its own and first specific task, questions about the deeply human meaning of energy production, distribution, and use.

This is why the management of energy requires great wisdom and prudence, as well as a sense of responsibility, in order to ensure the common good of all peoples, through ethical and cultural interventions by public institutions, business enterprises, and organizations of civil society.

However, even individuals retain their own responsibility to follow the law present in their heart and recognized by reason. This natural law "is universal in its precepts and its authority extends to all men. It expresses the dignity of the person and determines the basis for his fundamental rights and duties."[37] Benedict XVI invites us to "listen to the language of nature and [to] answer accordingly,"[38] explaining that man is not self-creating freedom and that his will is righteous when he respects nature.

2. The Principle of Justice in Its Various Articulations

The principle of *justice*, articulated in its commutative, contributive, distributive aspects, namely as social justice,[39] must inspire, in particular, the search for solutions to the energy issue, helping to identify the path toward access to "modern" and sustainable energy for all. Justice leads to the hoped-for change of paradigm, and it can enlighten the UN principle of "*common but differentiated responsibilities.*"

Subjected to the regulation of the principle of justice is the equitable subdivision of the investments necessary for the development and promotion of access to energy. Developing countries and emerging economies must contribute thereto, in proportion to their possibilities, thus complementing traditional givers. For their part, advanced countries must concur thereto to a greater extent, as they have long benefited from large amounts of energy for their development and have long borne the primary responsibility for environmental degradation.

The principle of justice must also help to identify the damage caused by energy extraction and consumption processes, and to propose possible remedies or sanctions. Courts of justice, empowered to receive complaints presented by those whose environment or social rights have been violated, appear to be function for this purpose.

Likewise, the principle of justice should also guide the equitable distribution of energy and the related resources, such as water. In this regard, we point out that there are minimum levels of essential conditions for a decent existence, which are moreover not guaranteed in many developing countries, levels that must be satisfied prior to the very high levels of consumption, typical of more developed countries. "It is important to establish a real distributive justice"[40] that ensures that every person benefits, in a fair way, from the economic consequences of the exploitation of energy resources.

Justice, in harmony with the principle of subsidiarity, must rule in all spheres, from local to cross-border, from regional to national, from continental to international. Like solidarity, it must be *inter-* and *intra-generational. For this reason, in respect for those who will come after us, we "are not morally free to repeat the errors made in the past by others."*[41]

Since it must safeguard the right of all and especially of the weakest among us, justice urges the consideration that certain policies of forcefully imposed birth control are not a fair solution. In fact, they compel poorer communities to condition their population growth to allow other societies to maintain their current consumption.

3. An Approach in the Light of Subsidiarity

The *principle of subsidiarity*,[42] recalled by Benedict XVI in his encyclical *Caritas in veritate*, finds application in the field of energy in relation to development and is fundamental to any discussion about governance. The principle of subsidiarity means, *inter alia*, the right way to consider issues of global governance, specifying which matters need to be harmonized and managed at the global, national, regional, or local level. The policies that include the so-called "global commons," on the basis of which the results obtained by each country are not determined by internal policies, but by the total sum of the policies of other countries, cannot be left to individual states. Emissions of greenhouse gases and energy service represent the archetype of this principle. In the context of those policies, there are excellent reasons to establish binding global rules, since each country would have an interest in not contributing adequately to the maintenance of these "global commons," if left to act undisturbed. Furthermore, any failure to reach a global agreement would condemn us all to collective disaster.

The Principle

"In development programs, the principle of the centrality of the human person, as the subject primarily responsible for development, must be preserved. The principal concern must be to improve the actual living conditions of the people in a given region, thus enabling them to carry out those duties which their poverty does not presently allow them to fulfil. Social concern must never be an abstract attitude. Development programs, if they are to be adapted to individual situations, need to be flexible; and the people who benefit from them ought to be directly involved in their planning and implementation. The criteria to be applied should aspire towards incremental development in a context of solidarity—with careful monitoring of results—inasmuch as there are no universally valid solutions. Much depends on the way programs are managed in practice. 'The peoples themselves have the prime responsibility to work for their own development. But they will not bring this about in isolation' (*Populorum progressio*, no. 77). These words of Paul VI are all the more timely nowadays, as our world becomes progressively more integrated.

The dynamics of inclusion are hardly automatic. Solutions need to be carefully designed to correspond to people's concrete lives, based on a prudential evaluation of each situation. Alongside macro-projects, there is a place for micro-projects, and above all there is need for the active mobilization of all the subjects of civil society, both juridical and physical persons."[43]

Subsidiarity, understood in the positive sense as economic, institutional, or juridical assistance offered to the smallest social entities, entails a corresponding series of negative implications that require higher levels—such as the international community in relation to the state, or the state for the local level—to refrain from anything what would *de facto* restrict the existential space of the smaller essential cells of society. Their freedom, responsibility, and effective initiatives must not be supplanted.[44]

With regard to economically less advanced societies, it must be added that it is not legitimate to act *a priori* or imprudently against the whole of customs and traditions proper to the community, in cases where it plays an important role in the universal destination of goods.[45] Moreover, no context must be considered too poor, isolated, or unprofitable not to "deserve" investments and efforts for its development. It is precisely because of this that private and public investments should be encouraged with appropriate, fiscal, credit and security policies, so that they can be sufficiently guaranteed to increase the flourishing of initiatives. It is also necessary to hinder the onset of underdevelopment cycles in poorer areas or the prolonged control by criminal organizations harmful to economy and civil society. The key issue is, therefore, to find gradual solutions to reduce illegality and violence, which prevent development in these areas. Finally, financial strategies, international investment policies, and big development projects must be balanced and inspired by a preferential option for the poor:[46] it is not morally acceptable to force the governments of less wealthy countries to accept unfair conditions that are, however, extremely beneficial to those who own technology and capital.

Practical Application: Toward the Sustainability of Cities

Urbanization policies and programs that take due account of low-cost production and distribution of energy are required at all relevant levels.

The consumption of energy and fuels in urban areas must be reduced[47] and at the same time alternative modes of *in loco* energy production must be sought and promoted. This will increase the sustainability of cities and reduce their external dependence and their vulnerability to sudden phenomena.

Aware of the huge amount of urban waste, among the various avenues of research, we particularly encourage studies on waste recycling and the production of energy from waste processing. Further energy savings can result from the adoption of differentiated circuits for drinking water and water not suitable for direct use.

Practical Application: Toward Rural Electrification

The lack of infrastructure in underdeveloped rural areas, which has been discussed previously, should be addressed seriously. Governments, credit institutions, and international organizations are required to cooperate with each other to bring about, as soon as possible, the essential qualitative leap in the standard of living represented by the supply of electrical energy. This can indeed mark the dividing line between underdevelopment and development.

The answer to this lack can be sought in two different interventions, one normative and one technical. This involves defining appropriate development policies at the local level and adopting distributed generation systems.

The definition and adoption of policies for the promotion and development of electricity is the method followed historically in industrial countries, so that electrification did not only reach big urban areas and industrial centers but also rural and less populated areas. For this purpose, between the 1930s and the 1960s of last century, governments in advanced countries defined and implemented rural electrification programs that did not fail to produce positive results, transferring the higher costs incurred to the community.

While this model can be implemented in developing countries, it can effectively be combined with the adoption of distributed generation systems, based on correct and already mentioned mixes of renewable and non-renewable energy resources. Such systems must be carefully designed, as regards technologies and sources used, on the basis of the particular conditions existing at the local level. In particular, distributed generation can be a solution in very isolated areas, where it is possible and convenient to build small generators connected to micro-grids for the distribution of electrical energy, easy to finance, construct, manage, and keep operating. These solutions include, for example, wind turbines, efficient systems for the combustion of wood or other biomasses, and small hydroelectric systems. Modern technologies now offer easily replicable solutions, which can be applied on a small scale. They require specific training and can be designed in order to encourage the creation of jobs and to bring economic benefits to communities in the long term, in addition to those offered directly by electricity.

In certain cases, it might be appropriate to reduce the need for electricity as much as possible and, even more, to avoid stalemate in the development process, waiting for expected but distant electrification. Therefore, the use of simple mechanical or thermal devices must be encouraged, as it will be later explained.

It should be noted that certain decentralized solutions still prove too expensive when numerous populations are to be supplied with electricity. Extensive networks and big power plants have demonstrated their low-cost effectiveness in large urban areas and in relation to certain energy sources. However, the future development of distributed energy is likely to have a gradually greater role in metropolitan areas as well.

A Call for Responsibility in the Conception of New Projects

Allowing real development according to the principle of sub-sidiarity does not "only" mean supplying energy, but also respecting the dignity of people who are thus accompanied and made protagonists in the path toward access to energy and a better standard of living.

Therefore, practices and policies that do tend to provide new energy solutions but do not respect final users or the people concerned are to be avoided. An example is given by projects that exclude the necessary preliminary studies to assess whether the presumed solution is the most suitable for the type of community to be helped, or that minimize or dissimulate the negative impact on local communities, on their environment and on their way of life. Likewise, programs that disregard informing users or, even worse, are driven only by the logic of profit for profit's sake should be disapproved of. For example, the installation of solar panels in little developed areas without constant monitoring and suitable training will lead to the misuse and the prompt non-use thereof. Similar installations will only benefit entrepreneurs and contribute to the squandering of both funds intended for development and natural resources invested in manufacturing.

4. Solidarity between States

The improvement of the world balances seems to be increasingly connected to the application of a solidarity-based development model, which can reconcile and meet the progress expectations of both rich countries and poor ones. Given its pervasiveness and importance, the field of energy production, transport, and use is the one in which a solidarity-based development model could find more immediate and unambiguous application, but is also the one in which, as observed in the past, it is more difficult to intervene. Therefore, there is an urgent need for "a new solidarity, especially in relations between the developing nations and those that are highly industrialized"[48] and toward the youngest and most vulnerable peoples that "are asking that they be allowed to take part in the construction of a better world."[49]

On the basis of the reflections conducted at numerous venues, the success of the solidarity-based model in the field of energy assumes that the development of energy systems is regulated by the application of certain basic principles:

- advanced countries have the moral duty of supporting the transfer to less developed countries of the necessary know-how to use the energy resources essential to their development in an effective and sustainable way;
- the resort to the most complex energy technologies by advanced countries is aimed at limiting or reducing their demand for—and therefore the consequent economic pressure on—energy sources that are easier to use, in order to make them accessible to poorer countries at sustainable costs. Accordingly, the former have the moral duty of developing the use of the most complex and capital-intensive energy technologies, in order to allow the latter to feed their development, resorting to simpler and less expensive energy technologies.

IV. Technological Evolution

1. Hope and Encouragement

"Our civilization—above all its scientists and technicians—must look for new methods to use the sources of energy that Divine Providence has put at the disposal of man."[50] Technology and scientific progress aimed at guaranteeing increasingly better and at least decent standards of living and consumption can offer a manifold contribution toward solving the energy issue. As Paul VI explained, "the scientist must be animated by the confidence that nature has in store secret possibilities, which it is up to intelligence to discover and make use of, in order to reach the development which is in the Creator's plan. This hope in the Author of nature and of the human spirit, rightly understood, is capable of giving new and serene energy to the researcher who is a believer."[51] Moreover, there are intrinsic grounds for hope in the fact that "technology—it is worth emphasizing—is a profoundly human reality, linked to the autonomy and freedom of man. In technology we express and confirm the hegemony of the spirit over matter. The human spirit, 'increasingly free of its bondage to creatures, can be more easily drawn to the worship and contemplation of the Creator' (*Populorum progressio*, no. 41)."[52]

A glimmer of hope is, first of all, the research into alternative, renewable forms of energy applicable in different contexts and on different scales: forms of energy that preserve the heritage of creation and minimize risks to humanity.[53] In particular, it is desirable that this research offers "effective ways of exploiting the immense potential of solar energy,"[54] along with new methods of utilization of biomasses, biogases, the wind, and other natural elements. These methods will contribute to the progressive reduction of the demand for fossil energy and, of course, they will have to be studied and be applicable to various technological and socioeconomic levels. Therefore, it is necessary to address the problems of intermittence in the supply of energy, typical of certain renewable sources, and to invest in technologies and infrastructure for transport and storage. In this sense, encouragement needs to be given to the study of increasingly competitive, safe, and efficient methods of using hydrogen in the field of energy.

It is likewise required to support the search for greater energy efficiency, in order to save resources: innovations that make for maximum energy from every drop of oil and every gram of coal seem to be particularly useful, like those that favor the recovery and reuse of heat produced during certain transformation processes. There is also a need to develop technologies to bring down the cost of energy—for example, by simplifying its management or production—and to reduce the negative impact on the environment and on human health.[55]

As already mentioned, technology must also make a vital contribution to the supply of energy in two diametrically opposed areas: megalopolises, inhabited by tens of millions of people, and isolated rural areas. In this regard, the attention to the poorest demands that encouragement be given to technical or procedural innovations that represent effective and accessible energy options for less developed contexts that still lack electricity, where millions of people live, especially farming families and communities. Better harnesses or yokes ensure increased effectiveness of animals used for plowing or transport, and consequently better exploitation of their energy; solar dryers for the conservation of fruit, vegetables, etc.; mechanical pumps, such as pedal-powered ones, to draw water for irrigation a few meters deep: these are all modest but effective improvements.

For all these reasons, countries should be encouraged to work together and to harmonize scientific cooperation and the diffusion of technology and know-how, with a proper management of patents. In fact, "energy cooperation should ultimately be oriented toward poverty alleviation and be adjusted to […] transfer of technologies and best practices in this field,"[56] since their access by developing countries is essential to meet their growing demand, without compromising the ecosystem.

2. Prudence and Security

In the research into new technologies and in the studies for their application, the fundamental laws of nature must absolutely be taken into account. We must be particularly aware of the *principle of entropy*, which refers to the irreversibility of all the processes that occur in nature. This irreversibility demands greater and greater responsibility toward each human action. This, in energy management, leads us to consider the *principle of minimization* of all forms of environmental impact. Therefore, we must constantly be guided by the *precautionary principle*, thus stated: *in all human activities related to nature and to future generations, it is necessary to take the due precautions in order not to cause damage, especially long-term or irreversible.*

The precautionary principle is necessary in the context of technological and energy progress, because the new discoveries must be applied only after adequate studies on feasibility and sustainability for societies, economies, and the environment. Unfortunately, we have often witnessed the fact that the indiscriminate application of certain technological and scientific discoveries over time has produced harmful effects.[57]

Finally, we point out that technology has limits, in the sense that:

- not all that is feasible is morally acceptable, and for this reason technology must be accompanied and guided by valid ethical principles;[58]
- the production of energy, no matter how renewable and modern it may be, always starts from a nontechnological natural resource (water, waves, wind, sun, etc.) that escapes human control;
- tomorrow's technology may not be able to remedy today's damage;
- the hoped-for and expected evolution of technology might come too late for humanity to escape the negative consequences of current irresponsible behavior. Moreover, any technological innovation needs physiological time to spread and be able to significantly satisfy a primary need.

Still following the above-mentioned precautionary principle, we encourage the promotion and adoption of safety and monitoring measures during production, transport, and use of energy. It is indeed essential for a society to be able to ensure the security of each of the energy forms that constitute its mix, and to make serious efforts to this end. Security requires the adoption of appropriate technical and legal measures, as well as action and responses at the cultural and ethical level. There is also a strong need for preventive measures, training programs, and special codes of conduct for the personnel, who must always be responsible for the possible effects of the activities carried out. Security depends both on States and on the sense of responsibility of each person.[59]

It is therefore necessary to thoroughly consider both the risks and the possibilities offered by recent discoveries, by new technologies or processes, in areas to which researchers currently target their efforts. Certain points of the energy question, on which attention, investment, hopes, and controversy are often focused, must be examined with particular care.

One of these is surely the "non-conventional" gas known by the term *shale gas*, obtained from particular rocky formations called clay shales. In recent years, this source of fuel supply has been the subject of research in various areas of the world, especially in the United States, some European countries, and China, since the environmental consequences of its extraction arouse concerns.

Aware of the reality represented today by the increased number of nuclear power plants and States that intend to have their own, we finally insist—as the diplomacy of the Holy See often does—on how essential safety measures are in this particular sector.

V. Energy, Ethics, and Education

"The seriousness of the ecological issue lays bare the depth of man's moral crisis. If an appreciation of the value of the human person and of human life is lacking, we will also lose interest in others and in the earth itself,"[60] stated Saint John Paul II. In fact, humanity and the environment are closely linked to each other. At the beginning of this reflection on ethics and education, we would like to give an easily comprehensible example: laws or institutions will probably never prohibit or punish the use of a jeep to go to buy a superfluous item in a store round the corner, perhaps leaving lights and taps on in the temporarily empty house, regardless of the fact that, somewhere else, somebody does not have enough energy or water to live with an ounce of dignity. *Only ethical education can prevent similar aberrant behavior.*

1. The Need for a Valid Ethical Approach

"The entire socio-cultural system, by ignoring the ethical and religious dimension, has been weakened, and ends by limiting itself to the production of goods and services alone."[61] The absence of valid and shared ethical foundations can be perceived in the inadequacy of human actions regarding both the environment and energy and the legislative process and the creation of institutions.

Ethical principles are essential to establish a hierarchy of values and priorities, and set up behavior patterns.

Especially today, the dominant ethics is essentially centered on the pursuit of profit for profit's sake and seems to be the only motive underlying the decisions and behavior of most governors, opinion formers like the media, and business managers. Moved by such ethics, they cannot promote human dignity, foster the integral development of peoples, or change the energy paradigm. A further source of serious concern, also of an ethical nature, is the persistence of financial economy that is an end unto itself, destined therefore to contradict its goals, since it is no longer in touch with its roots and has lost sight of its constitutive purpose, namely its original and essential role of serving the real economy and, ultimately, of serving the development of people and the human community.[62]

We urgently need a conversion of hearts and minds to new values, to a valid ethical approach.

"Love, often restricted to relationships of physical closeness or limited to merely subjective aspects of action on behalf of others, must be reconsidered in its authentic value as the highest and universal criterion of the whole of social ethics."[63] Love must be associated with universal destination of goods, solidarity, and participation, so that peoples are no longer passive tools but they become the protagonists of their future.[64] A fundamental element is the connection between moral order and legal order, which leads to the awareness of the intrinsic ethical dimension of every social and political issue.[65] This series of ethical elements is concluded by the awareness of the "limit," emblematic of the human condition, to be admitted and accepted. Let us think of the limit in technology: not everything that is technically feasible is morally acceptable. There is also a limit in economies and in the environment: we cannot expect to produce and consume more and more, beyond measure, forgetting that we depend on the resources of creation.

With this ethical approach, it will be possible to pursue an integral development of all peoples that does not damage creation, but preserves and cultivates it as much as possible for the good of all mankind. *This is the approach that must guide the action of governors, media, and educators, who in turn are required to promote it.*

This ethical approach, in particular, would cause governors to acknowledge that the energy issue and the development challenge demand urgent action, as it is no longer acceptable to merely express principles and make statements. It would also be a basis for admitting that it is irrelevant to give occasional financial aids to less developed countries without seriously committing to the ethical reorganization of the most advanced and consuming economies. Such humanistic awareness would boost the implementation of the necessary changes.

Finally, this valid ethical approach should also guide the research and application of technology. As John Paul II explained, "if humanity today succeeds in combining the new scientific capacities with a strong ethical dimension, it will certainly be able to promote the environment as a home and a resource for man and for all men"[66] and consequently, to ensure access to "modern" and sustainable energy for all.

2. Education Is Fundamental

Education with an eye to ethics, respecting the natural moral law it derives from, must be imparted to the whole of civil society and to every person. We must educate ourselves "in compassion, solidarity, working together,"[67] altruism, responsibility, social justice, and trans-nationality, namely the idea of brotherhood or global citizenship. Education must mold righteous people, respectful of human dignity, with strong sensitivity to the common good and the public good of access to energy; people aware of the consequences that their actions can have on others and on the environment. Ultimately, education with an eye to ethics contributes to develop the sensitivity and the will to participate in the integral development and, therefore, in the sound management of energy.

The youth, in particular, must be educated to justice and peace, as Benedict XVI advocated in his *Message of the World Day of Peace 2012*. It seems particularly important to educate the new generations to overcome the idea of indiscriminate consumption as an indication of development and social affluence, which are played up as the ultimate truth by certain economic models. Only if educated to a responsible and cautious use, will the youth be able to perceive energy sobriety not as impoverishment, but as a real opportunity for growth in awareness, solidarity, and therefore humanity.

The *need for education* will never be replaced by the adoption of technical measures or by the creation of institutions, no matter how refined and advanced they may be. Ethical education is an enormous responsibility of States, media, families, and the whole of civil society.

Even the Church can make, how and where possible, in its cultural and educational institutions and through its apostolic activity, a valuable contribution toward creating a suitable culture and teaching, by combining the spread of the Gospel message with a human teaching, intended to raise awareness of the impact of individuals and communities' actions on creation, even in terms of energy and environment.

CHAPTER 4

Concrete Proposals

Following the foregoing considerations, it is natural to call on the entire international community, States, local authorities, companies, political and scientific leaders, together with all the people of good will, to take due account of the following proposals.

1. Change of the Energy Paradigm: Acting Quickly in the Name of Solidarity

The necessary change of the energy paradigm must ensure that everybody is provided with enough energy for a decent life. It is therefore desirable that the players in the energy sector sincerely commit to guarantee, in the shortest time and for the largest number of people possible, access to sustainable energy that complies with the conditions listed above.

We here reiterate the heartfelt appeal of the Pastoral Constitution *Gaudium et spes*, which, citing the judgment of the Ancient Fathers "feed the man dying of hunger, because if you have not fed him, you have killed him," urges all, according to the ability of each, to provide the peoples with the aid by which they may be able to help and develop themselves.[1] For this reason, in negotiations about energy, in the functioning of international institutions, in the social responsibility of companies, there is an urgent need for "a new solidarity, especially in relations between the developing nations and those that are highly industrialized,"[2] as well as within one country.

A proposal to be promoted and supported is, for example, that of the so-called *economy of communion*,[3] in which productive citizens—employers, employees, and other business figures—are inspired by principles rooted in a culture different from the one that prevails today in the economic practice and theory: a *culture of giving*, strongly antithetical to the *culture of having*, in which *economic giving* becomes an expression of *giving oneself on a human level* and reveals an anthropological conception that is nonindividualistic, non-collectivistic, but communal.

Specifically, intolerable situations of energy shortage must be solved in the short term and resilience capacities must be strengthened where the deterioration of the environment and the climate, related to the use of energy, is likely to worsen already difficult living conditions. A correct formulation of *precautionary principle* must guide decisions to the adoption of measures to mitigate polluting emissions, when economic and social costs are not excessive. At the same time, a serious conversion to solidarity-based and sustainable behavior must be politically conceived and started.

The world economy must gradually realize that, also in the coming decades, it will still depend mainly on energy sources that generate or exacerbate conflicts, and consequently it will have to adopt the necessary government measures and make the necessary reorientation choices. This evolution calls for will and perseverance—as policies in favor of human development, stability, peace, climate, and environment may bear fruit only in the long term—and it will surely require considerable and prolonged efforts. States, which have proved to be able to mobilize huge sums to bail out financial institutions deemed indispensable, will surely be able to find the necessary funds to effectively and efficiently secure peace, protect the environment and its resources,[4] and to ensure the change of the energy paradigm.

2. Sound Energy Mixes

Peoples must be able to gradually gain access to all those energy sources and technologies that they can manage appropriately along their socio-economic, technological, and industrial development path.

Therefore, with a view to the universal destination of *goods and in compliance with sustainability requirements, all energy resources available in nature must be usable by man without unjustified exceptions*, which have the effect of limiting choices and reducing the overall amount of resources available for the development of humanity. Every energy system must diversify the use of the resources available as much as possible, in order to reduce the social vulnerabilities associated with the depletion or sudden changes in the price of the various resources.

With the due control by public authorities and through the evolution of technology, mixes of various energy sources can be adopted according to the various contexts.

A joint effort must be directed to identifying, in the various situations, forms of energy that can be used in a sustainable way in terms of technology, economy, society, environment, and safety.

Hence, each context should find its own balance, its own mix, as harmonious as possible: powerful plants and big electrical grids on the one hand, distributed generation systems for mainly local consumption on the other hand.

3. Favoring the Micro Level

We have seen that, in line with the *principle of subsidiarity*, adequate local solutions must be promoted and developed where possible. In addition, various *microfinance* practices have already proved their effectiveness in the sector of energy. These must be encouraged, since they are accessible sources of credit for local projects and disadvantaged communities. *Microcredit*, which after a term ensures autonomy for these communities, is very positive, as it facilitates the appropriation of the project and generates a special sense of responsibility in all the people involved, by increasing their interest and pride in a shared endeavor.

"This inevitably needs the involvement of local institutions, which can more easily identify the type of energy, including the forms of financing and marketing most appropriate for the complex realities of the zone."[5]

Appropriate forms of credit, together with adequate policies and effective monitoring bodies, are the requirements for the development of small entrepreneurs in the field of energy. These players are particularly useful in less developed areas, where big companies providing energy services struggle to expand their networks.[6]

On the same line of action, efforts to fight indoor pollution must then be encouraged.

4. Ambitious Goals

New energy goals are required. These must be ambitious, set at the global level, and at the same time, they must make for the widest possible participation of the various social players.

These goals must guide development and aim at preserving the environment and boosting economies.

In particular, employment and business opportunities offered by sustainable, renewable, and alternative energy sources and by recycling in its various components must be highlighted and exploited. Suitable formation should be provided where necessary, along with targeted incentive policies.

The ambitious but realistic objective of the international energy policy, inspired by gratuitousness, is to allow every person to be able to procure a sufficient amount of energy for their sustenance and integral development toward a decent life.

5. More and More Renewable Energy

"Progress in the field of renewable energy is extremely important for poverty eradication. The many benefits of the application and dissemination of new and renewable sources of energy can be used for development related objectives."[7] It is necessary to pursue sustainable development based more on renewable energy sources than on non-renewable energy ones.

Emissions of carbon dioxide must be reduced in order to obtain a significant *decarbonization* of energy, economies, consumption, and production processes as much as possible.[8] This journey is long and gradual, but it should be undertaken with resolution,[9] given its importance for every single territory and for the whole world. For this purpose, private and public investments should be made into systems that produce less carbon dioxide or capture it; at the same time effective and fair carbon markets should be established.[10]

Moreover, fossil energy, despite repeated and expected cost increases, appears to be and to remain, on average, economically less expensive than renewable energy.[11]

This may discourage investment and private initiative in the search, development, and spreading of renewable energy sources. It is up to the public sector, where necessary, to support the development of renewable energy sources at lower prices, through investments and appropriate policies. What is at stake is environmental sustainability, security, geopolitical stability, and respect for societies.

It is encouraging that various countries are already aiming at identifying and adopting sustainable forms of energy. In the change of the energy paradigm and especially for this proposal and the following one, advanced countries clearly play a leading role that must "drive the change."

6. Sobriety

We are called on to live in this world with sobriety and fairness,[12] as already urged by the Apostles. "The principle of responsibility to the present generation and those to come [leads us to the] need to re-examine the models of consumption and production, often unsustainable."[13]

We cannot assume development goals and plan future economic growths, or even hope to maintain a *status quo* in consumption, without admitting that certain lifestyles are irresponsible and, consequently, without taking courageous and appropriate corrective measures, especially against waste. Even talking to those who live in abundance, Jesus Christ teaches that we should make sure that "nothing be wasted."[14]

We should then promote reasonable, responsible, and targeted sobriety objectives. The growing awareness about the global demand for energy must be followed by "an effective shift in mentality which can lead to the adoption of new lifestyles in which the quest for truth, beauty, goodness and communion with others for the sake of common growth are the factors which determine consumer choices, savings and investments."[15] Therefore, responsibility, "simplicity, moderation and discipline, as well as a spirit of sacrifice, must become a part of everyday life, lest all suffer the negative consequences of the careless habits of a few."[16]

The concern for the dignity and well-being of the human person pertains to any reflection on energy, justice, and peace. Therefore, we cannot ignore that the problems of energy overconsumption and overexploitation of natural resources can also be mitigated by the action of individuals, who would become physically more active, especially those who use a lot of power for private means of transport. Governments, media, and educational institutions should encourage and promote physical activity. As a matter of fact, the human body was created by God as a structure capable of absorbing, transforming, producing, and consuming energy.

Thus, the use of human energy for fitness or a bike would integrate the series of initiatives intended to cope with high energy consumption. Furthermore, it would help to solve the global problem of obesity and health care costs associated with it.

7. The Participation of Civil Society

The ongoing increase in the environmental and energy awareness of civil society must be supported. Moreover, inclusive processes in the resolution of the energy question must be encouraged. Citizens must not give up their primary responsibility, but they should support, where necessary, the production of sustainable energy plans by the authorities and require a good energy management from them. In fact, "civil society maintains the ultimate responsibility and so when the political community does not appear to be capable of carrying out its task, civil society has to get mobilized to make this happen."[17]

8. Recognizing Energy as a Prerequisite for Various Human Rights

Access to energy is a prerequisite for the enjoyment of most human rights. The promotion of the "fundamental human rights [along with] social progress and better standards of life"[18] logically implies the promotion of access to energy. Consequently, this assumes that it is accessible to every single person. In fact, "everyone has the right to a standard of living adequate for the health and well-being of himself."[19] This, in turn, implies the right to have a share of earthly goods sufficient for one's needs and those of one's family.[20] After all, the states involved in the United Nations Framework Convention on Climate Change (UNFCCC), as mentioned earlier, have already explicitly acknowledged that energy is indispensable to the development of each country.

Reflecting on the indispensability of access to energy is a way to recognize human dignity more effectively, to promote it universally, as a characteristic given to every person by God the Creator.[21]

The energy needed for a decent life should not be taken away from anyone, either by acts of terrorism, or by war, poverty, political will, speculation, or economic interests.

For these reasons, we hope that the reflection on the importance of energy at the international level will continue. Among the results of this reflection, we hope that:

1. public and private leaders will acknowledge that the satisfaction of basic energy needs is essential to the enjoyment of many other human rights, for an acceptable standard of living, for development and stability;
2. the poorer will develop and strengthen the conviction

that they are entitled to demand the satisfaction of their primary needs as a priority;

3. the international community and technical agencies will identify consensual minimum standards of energy.

9. An International Structure for Effective Governance

This governance should be able to act where the complex cross-border issues or the limitations of a single state make the pursuit of sustainable development for the environment and the human family particularly difficult. To this end, there is an urgent need for effective global governance for energy. It will have to be created and supported by the political will of every single government, provided with appropriate means to carry out its task—including technical-scientific resources—and conceived in such a way as to be able to easily cooperate with other international structures about energy-related activities.

This governance has the essential duty of regulating the extraction and trade of energy resources, especially those that have long been the subject of opaque international circuits and involve incompetent or corrupted public administrations, powerful multinational companies, as well as methods of obtaining and managing concessions that only just border on legality.[22] In particular, the following negative and immoral externalities of the energy sector must be opposed: speculation, illicit enrichment of a few, violations of the human rights of many, maintenance of unfair trading that consolidates non-development dynamics in the areas of origin of resources, unbalanced tax exemption policies;[23] irresponsible or long concealed acts of environmental degradation.

10. A Better Management of Resources

Policies, technologies, cooperation procedures, and development projects that ensure an improved management of natural resources must be encouraged. In particular, the following areas seem to be essential with regard to the energy question: assessment of the impact of energy production and use on water, assessment of the competition between the use of soils for energy or for food, search for increasingly greater efficiency and safety in biomass combustion, sustainable management of forests, search for new sources of energy, especially renewable ones.

Two examples of the issues involved can be mentioned. The first concerns the need to monitor economic aids in the sector of liquid biofuels with discernment. Incentives intended to favor the emergence of new initiatives must be maintained and encouraged, while subsidies—when becoming protectionist measures by advanced countries—should be reduced, or rather avoided. Ultimately, biofuels require more studies[24] and a good strict management, according to the *principle of prudence*, which must also regulate the use of liquid biofuels by future generations. Moreover, the replacement of food agriculture with energy agriculture has ethical and moral implications that require careful consideration, and it should motivate adequate governance, both at the international and national level. Considering the need to meet mankind's growing demand for food and energy, and in the light of current trends, it is advisable, in case of uncertainty, to give priority to the use of agricultural resources for food.

Finally, another example concerns the dual awareness of the need to treat contaminated water, as well as of the fact that not all waste water must necessarily be purified so as to become (again) drinking water. For example, water, at certain "intermediate levels of treatment"—which correspond to water, not polluted to the point of being dangerous for the environment, but still not drinkable—is a precious resource for irrigation, toilets, or cleaning. Identifying and planning human activities that make use of nonpotable water can reduce energy consumption for purification and allow better reuse of this essential element.

CHAPTER 5

Conclusion

The environment must be regarded as the real common heritage of mankind.[1] The protection of creation is a moral duty for all. The Creator wanted "men and women to be worthy of their vocation, managing nature not as ruthless exploiters but as responsible stewards."[2]

"Only by means of a common commitment to sharing is it possible to respond to the great challenge of our times: to build a world of peace and justice where each person can live with dignity. This can be achieved if a world model of authentic solidarity prevails which assures to all inhabitants of the planet food, water, necessary medical treatment, and also work and energy resources as well as cultural benefits, scientific and technological knowledge,"[3] a world where every woman and every man benefit from real development. "An education in ecological responsibility is urgent: responsibility for oneself, for others, and for the earth."[4]

Changing behavior, markets, and policies in a short time and in a radical way is difficult. Especially when, beyond the immediacy of the present, such "immediate" systems—in the sense that they basically react to immediate stimuli and with a view to immediate results—must be changed for the well-being of a future world, which is not always clearly perceptible, in order to avoid or at least prudently mitigate the probable catastrophic environmental consequences of a future that often appears deceptively distant. Now, "help" toward undertaking these changes is offered by religions, since many of them—especially the Christian faith open to Transcendence—are characterized by a special perception of time. It is a wide perception, which incorpo-rates gratitude for the current life received and the hope for the future. This perception offers those who share it the energy and will-ingness to change, even though it is burdensome, even though it is aimed to obtain benefits for distant generations. Openness to Tran-scendence also infuses deep respect for nature, which is perceived as a precious gift from the Creator, and so it counteracts the recurring human temptation to "dominate" nature while damaging it. More-over, the eschatological dimension of Christianity is an incentive to steer the ethical question about energy toward a teleological direc-tion: only by looking at a "future" that, as we know, is already given, the eschatological Christ, can and must we build it through really prophetic views and attitudes.

Hence, it can be considered "a duty of justice and charity to make a resolute and persevering effort to husband energy resources and respect nature, so that not only humanity as a whole today may benefit, but also the generations to come."[5]

We are aware of the fact that energy injustice, competition for natural resources, and climatic evolutions can produce suffering on a large scale. We must, therefore, work out a real and global develop-ment plan to manage an essential good like energy with justice: this is an indispensable requirement for peace between peoples.[6]

Notes

Preface

1. Benedict XVI, *Address to the General Assembly of the United Nations*, New York, April 18, 2008.

2. Benedict XVI, Encyclical letter *Caritas in veritate* (June 29, 2009), in *AAS* 101 (2009): 641–709, no. 50.

Chapter 1

1. John Paul II, Encyclical letter *Centesimus annus* (May 1, 1991), in *AAS* 83 (1991)/2: 793–867, no. 5.

2. John Paul II, Encyclical letter *Sollicitudo rei socialis* (December 30, 1987), in *AAS* 80 (1988): 513–86, no. 4.

3. *Centesimus annus*, no. 29.

4. Cf. Paul VI, Encyclical letter *Populorum progressio* (March 26, 1967). For the English text and the numbering we follow, for convenience, D. J. O'Brien and T. A. Shannon, eds., *Catholic Social Thought: The Documentary Heritage* (Maryknoll, NY: Orbis Books, 1992), 240–60, nos. 14 and 42.

5. Cf. *Caritas in veritate*, no. 8.

6. Cf. Matt 5:45.

7. Cf. Matt 25:31–46.

8. Cf. *Caritas in veritate*, no. 36.

9. Cf. Gen 2:15.

10. Cf. Gen 2:9.

11. Cf. Second Vatican Ecumenical Council, Pastoral Constitution on the Church in the Modern World *Gaudium et spes* (December 7, 1965), in *AAS* 58 (1966): 1025–1115, no. 36.

12. Cf. *Catechism of the Catholic Church* (Vatican City: Libreria Editrice Vaticana, 2003), no. 302.

13. Francis, Encyclical letter *Lumen fidei* (June 29, 2013), in *AAS* 105 (2013): 555–96, no. 34.

14. Cf. *Centesimus annus*, no. 25.

15. Cf. *Caritas in veritate*, nos. 11 and 47.

16. Cf. Benedict XVI, *Easter Vigil Homily in the Holy Night*, April 7, 2012.

17. Cf. Benedict XVI, *Address on the Occasion of Christmas Greetings to the Roman Curia*, December 21, 2012.

18. Cf. Gen 2:15; Sir 17:2; Lev 25:23; Wis 49.

19. *Gaudium et spes*, no. 34.

20. Cf. Gen 2:15.

21. *Caritas in veritate*, no. 50.

22. Cf. Francis, *Homily, Holy Mass for the Beginning of the Petrine Ministry*, March 19, 2013; *Address to the General Audience*, June 5, 2013.

23. Paul VI, *Address for the Plenary Session of the Pontifical Academy of Sciences*, April 19, 1975.

24. Cf. Aristotle, *Metaphysics*, IX, 3, 1047 a 30s. *et passim*.

25. The concept of *continuity* is also important to compare all the usable sources: while fossil fuels and uranium can be generally considered as continuous sources, since the energy that they produce depends only on their exploitation, certain renewable sources (wind, sun, tides…) are instead typically discontinuous (also referred to as intermittent), because their availability is subject to factors beyond the control of man and therefore it makes the harmonious synthesis of energy availability and its use in a certain moment very important. The absence of solar energy on cloudy days or wind energy on windless days results in the need to resort to energy storage systems and other secondary sources in order to meet such consumption. The

use of solar energy for winter heating poses obvious problems when compared to its use in the summer.

26. These considerations are increasingly important when analyzing the use of renewable energy sources from an economic-political point of view. In fact, on the one hand, the diffusion of technologies for the exploitation of these sources presents fundamental environmental advantages; on the other hand, certain problematic features of these solutions start to emerge in the relationship with territories (compatibility of wind blades with the landscape, use of the territory for large photovoltaic parks with a reduction of areas intended for food crops, etc.).

27. They covered 81% in 2010. Cf. IEA, *World Energy Outlook 2011—Executive Summary* (2011), 2. This percentage seems destined to decrease very slowly, cf. IEA, *World Energy Investment Outlook. Special Report* (June 2014), 24.

28. Cf. International Strategy for Disaster Reduction, *Hyogo Framework for Action 2005–2015: Building the Resilience of Nations and Communities to Disasters* (Geneva, 2007).

29. Cf. World Bank, *Sustainable Energy for All: Global Tracking Framework* (2013), vol. III, 79.

30. John Paul II, *Address to Participants in the Study Week on "Energy and Humanity" of the Pontifical Academy of Sciences*, November 14, 1980.

31. Cf. *Gaudium et spes*, no. 33.

32. Animals are still fundamental in many agricultural areas, especially in Asia and Africa.

33. The European Coal and Steel Community (ECSC) and the International Atomic Energy Agency (IAEA) were established in the 1950s, after the Second World War. The International Energy Agency (IEA) was established in the 1970s in response to an oil crisis. Organizations such as the World Trade Organization (WTO), the Food and Agriculture Organization of the United Nations (FAO), and the Organization for Economic Cooperation and Development

(OECD) are more and more frequently concerned with energy, among other things and with different approaches.

34. Benedict XVI, Post-Synodal Apostolic Exhortation *Africae Munus* (November 19, 2011), in *AAS* 104 (2012): 239–314, no. 80.

Chapter 2

1. Cf. United Nations Conference on Trade and Development—UNCTAD, *Technology and Innovation Report 2011* (2011), *Overview*, xvi.

2. Cf. World Bank, *Sustainable Energy for All: Global Tracking Framework* (2013), vol. III, 38.

3. Cf. IEA/OECD, *World Energy Outlook 2012—Executive Summary* (2012), 7.

4. Cf. Pius XI, Encyclical letter *Quadragesimo anno* (May 15, 1931), in *AAS* 23 (1931): 177–228, no. 5.

5. Cf. *Caritas in veritate*, no. 50.

6. Hundreds of millions of people are waiting to gain access to the use of electricity: when they are allowed thereto, there will inevitably be an exponential increase of energy issues, and further challenges to development will come up, requiring new infrastructure for energy transportation and trade, new forms of use and sharing of primary energy resources, new criteria for more sustainable impact on the environment, the territory, and the landscape.

7. Cf. UN, *United Nations Framework Convention on Climate Change*, 1992.

8. Cf. UN—Secretary-General's High-Level Panel on Global Sustainability, *Resilient People, Resilient Planet: A Future Worth Choosing*, 2012, The Panel's vision, no. 7.

9. Cf. IEA, *Energy Use in the New Millennium*, 2007, pp. 101 and 120.

10. Cf. OECD, *Towards Green ICT Strategies*, June 2009, p. 7.

11. Cf. World Bank, *Striking a Better Balance—The Final Report of the Extractive Industries Review*, December 2003, vol. I, 5.

12. Cf. The Royal Society, *Climate Change: A Summary of the Science*, September 2010, pp. 1, 6 and 7; Pontifical Academy of Sciences, *Fate of Mountain Glaciers in the Anthropocene*, May 11, 2011, pp. 1 and 3.

13. The anthropogenic production of carbon dioxide is largely related to the use of fossil energy sources.

14. Cf. Pontifical Academy of Sciences, *Study Week on "A Modern Approach to the Protection of the Environment,"* Vatican City 1989, pp. 79 and 86.

15. Cf. IEA, *World Energy Outlook 2012—Executive Summary*, 2012, p. 4; Ibid., *Key World Energy Statistics 2012*, 2012, p. 10.

16. John Paul II, *Message for the World Day of Peace 1990*, no. 9.

17. For the consequences of corruption, cf. Pontifical Council For Justice And Peace, *The Fight against Corruption*, Vatican City 2006, nos. 3–5 and 11; Ibid., *Compendium of the Social Doctrine of the Church*, Vatican City 2004, no. 411.

18. Cf. Africa Progress Panel, *Equity in Extractives—Stewarding Africa's Natural Resources for All*, 2013, pp. 87 and 88.

19. On corporate responsibility in outsourcing and respect for the environment, cf. *Caritas in veritate*, no. 40.

20. Cf. FAO/OECD, *Agricultural Outlook 2013–2022*, 2013, p. 106.

21. Cf. FAO, *Right to Food and Bioenergy*, "Focus on Paper," 2007.

22. Cf. FAO, *State of the World's Forests 2009*, Rome 2009, p. 68; Ibid., *State of the World's Forests 2012*, Rome 2012, pp. 27 and 28.

23. Cf. IEA/OECD, *Energy for All—Financing Access for the Poor* (Special early excerpt of the *World Energy Outlook 2011*), October 2011, pp. 3 and 7.

24. Cf. FAO Wood Energy, http://foris.fao.org/preview/70066/en/ (consulted on July 10, 2014).

25. Cf. FAO, *Right to Food and Bioenergy*, "Focus on Paper," 2007.

26. Cf. FAO, *Global Forest Resources Assessment 2010 Main Report*, "Forestry Paper" 163, Rome 2010, p. 11.

27. John Paul II, *Address to the Participants in the Study Week Organized by the Pontifical Academy of Sciences*, May 18, 1990, no. 2.

28. Cf. FAO, *The State of Food and Agriculture in Asia and the Pacific Region 2008*, (Bangkok, 2008), 22.

29. Cf. FAO, *Unasylva*, vol. LIX 2008/1, pp. 2 and 12.

30. A rudimentary land fertilization technique that consists in burning vegetation or crop residues.

31. John Paul II, *Address to the Participants in the Study Week Organized by the Pontifical Academy of Sciences*, May 18, 1990, no. 3.

32. Cf. National Research Council, *Urban Pollution from Wood Combustion*, 2010, http://www.cnr.it/istituti/FocusByN_eng.html?cds=046&nfocus=6 (consulted on July 10, 2014).

33. Cf. World Health Organization, *WHO Guidelines for Indoor Air Quality: Selected Pollutants*, 2010, p. 1.

34. Cf. IEA, *Cities, Towns and Renewable Energy*, 2009, pp. 20ss.

35. Cf. UN-Habitat, *World Habitat Day 2011, Cities and Climate Change*, October 3, 2011, p. 11.

36. Cf. Holy See, *Intervention at the 46th Session of the General Conference of the International Atomic Energy Agency*, Vienna, September 17, 2002.

37. Cf. UN-HABITAT, *World Habitat Day 2011, Cities and Climate Change*, October 3, 2011, p. 3.

38. A similar analysis can be made about water.

39. United Nations General Assembly, Resolution: *International Year of Sustainable Energy for All*, 65/151, December 20, 2010.

40. Cf. FAO—Committee of Agriculture, *Bioenergy, Item 7 of the Provisional Agenda*, COAG/2005/7, December 2004, p. 1.

41. Cf. FAO, *The State of Food Insecurity in the World 2013*, Rome 2013, p. 8; Ibid., *The State of Food and Agriculture*, Rome 2013, p. 3.

42. Cf. FAO, *"Energy-Smart" Food for People and Climate— Issue Paper*, Rome 2011, p. 9.

43. Cf. FAO, *How to Feed the World in 2050*, October 2009, pp. 2 and 10.

44. Cf. FAO, *"Energy-Smart" Food for People and Climate— Issue Paper*, Rome 2011, p. 3.

45. Cf. FAO, *Global Food Losses and Food Waste*, Rome 2011, p. 4.

46. Francis, *Address to the General Audience*, June 5, 2013; Ibid., *Message for the World Food Day 2013*, October 16, 2013, no. 2.

47. Cf. Holy See, *Intervention at the 30th Session of FAO Regional Conference for Latina America and the Caribbean*, Brasilia, April 14–18, 2008, no. 8.

48. Benedict XVI, *Message to the Director General of FAO on the Occasion of World Food Day 2011*, October 17, 2011.

49. Benedict XVI, *Message to the Director General of FAO on the Occasion of World Food Day 2012*, October 16, 2012, no. 2.

50. Here, we only intend to analyze the *civil* or *peaceful aspect* of the discussion about nuclear power. In fact, the repeated condemnation by the Holy See of the development of nuclear weapons, their proliferation, their use, and its possible consequences is well known and is not subject to discussion or possible false interpretations, as will be seen hereinafter, cf. p. 66.

51. *The Treaty on the Non-Proliferation of Nuclear Weapons* of 1968 recognizes, in article IV.1, the inalienable right of all the parties to the Treaty to develop research, production, and use of nuclear energy for peaceful purposes. The Holy See has ratified this treaty. However, the Holy See does not consider this right as absolute but subject to the condition of a real process of complete and general disarmament. Cf. Holy See, *Intervention at the Ministerial Conference on Nuclear Energy in the 21st Century*, Beijing, April 21, 2009.

52. Cf. Holy See, *Intervention at the Ministerial Conference on Nuclear Energy in the 21st Century*, Beijing, April 21, 2009.

53. Cf. Holy See, *Intervention at the 57th General Conference of the International Atomic Energy Agency*, Vienna, September 16, 2013.

54. *Compendium of the Social Doctrine of the Church*, no. 447.

55. Cf. UNEP—United Nations Environment Program, *Towards a Green Economy; Pathways to Sustainable Development and Poverty Eradication*, 2011, Water chapter, pp. 16 and 17; World Bank, *Thirsty Energy*, Water papers 78923, June 2013, p. 9ff.

56. Cf. Pontifical Council For Justice And Peace, *Water, an Essential Element for Life—Contributions of the Holy See on Occasion of the World Water Forums*, Vatican City 2013, p. 94.

57. Cf. FAO/OECD, *Agricultural Outlook 2011–2020*, 2011, p. 88.

58. Francis, *Address to the New Ambassadors Accredited to the Holy See*, May 16, 2013.

59. Cf. John Paul II, *Message for the World Day of Peace 1999*, no. 9; Ibid., Encyclical letter *Redemptor Hominis* (March 4, 1979), in *AAS* 71 (1979): 257–324, no. 16; Francis, Apostolic Exhortation *Evangelii Gaudium* (November 24, 2013), in *AAS* 105 (2013): 1019–1137, no. 54.

60. Cf. *Centesimus annus*, no. 35.

61. Cf. *Caritas in veritate*, no. 40.

62. *Centesimus annus*, no. 29.

63. Cf. Benedict XVI, *Address to the New Ambassadors Accredited to the Holy See on the Occasion of the Presentation of the Letters of Credence*, December 17, 2009.

64. Cf. *Caritas in veritate*, no. 49.

65. Cf. Holy See, *Intervention at the 15th OSCE Ministerial Council*, Madrid, November 29, 2007.

66. Cf. John Paul II, *Message for the World Day of Peace 1990*, no. 1.

67. *Caritas in veritate*, no. 49.

68. John Paul II, *Address to the Members of the NATO Defense College*, July 12, 1982, no. 2.

69. Cf. Ibid., *Message for the World Day of Peace 1990*, no. 12.

Chapter 3

1. Cf. Benedict XVI, *Address on the Occasion of the Meeting with the Civil Authorities at Westminster Hall*, apostolic journey to the United Kingdom, September 17, 2010.

2. Cf. *Caritas in veritate*, no. 37; Pontifical Council for Justice and Peace, *Vocation of the Business Leader—A Reflection*, Vatican City, January 2013, p. 11.

3. Cf. *Quadragesimo anno*, no. 58.

4. *Centesimus annus*, no. 31.

5. Leo XIII, Encyclical letter *Rerum novarum* (May 15, 1891), in D. J. O'Brien and T. A. Shannon, eds., *Catholic Social Thought: The Documentary Heritage* (Maryknoll, NY:Orbis Books, 1992), 16.

6. *Gaudium et spes*, no. 69.

7. *Catechism of the Catholic Church*, no. 1905.

8. *Compendium of the Social Doctrine of the Church*, chap. 4.

9. *Gaudium et spes*, no. 26.

10. Cf. Pontifical Commission "Iustitia et Pax," *The Universal Purpose of Created Things*, Vatican City 1977.

11. John Paul II, *Address to Participants in the Study Week on "Energy and Humanity" of the Pontifical Academy of Sciences*, November 14, 1980.

12. Cf. United Nations General Assembly, Resolution: *International Year of Sustainable Energy for All*, 65/151, December 20, 2010, followed by the Resolution: *Promotion of New and Renewable Sources of Energy*, 67/215, December 21, 2012, which declares "2014–2024 the United Nations Decade of Sustainable Energy for All."

13. Cf. Benedict XVI, *Address on the Occasion of the Meeting with the Civil Authorities at Westminster Hall*, September 17, 2010.

14. Cf. *Compendium of the Social Doctrine of the Church*, no. 373.

15. Cf. *Populorum progressio*, no. 14.

16. Cf. Benedict XVI, *Address on the Meeting with the Civil Authorities at Westminster Hall*, September 17, 2010.

17. Cf. Pontifical Council for Justice and Peace, *Towards Reforming the International Financial and Monetary Systems in the Context of Global Public Authority*, LEV, Vatican City 2011.

18. Cf. Benedict XVI, *Message for the World Day of Peace 2011*, no. 12.

19. Cf. *Caritas in veritate*, no. 50.

20. On the necessary collaboration of the international community and its responsibilities, cf. John Paul II, *Message for the World Day of Peace*, 1990, nos. 6, 9, and 15.

21. Holy See, *Intervention at the Ministerial Conference of the International Atomic Energy Agency on Nuclear Safety*, June 21, 2011. Still on the need for global governance, cf. Holy See, *Intervention at the General Debate of the 67th Session of the United Nations General Assembly*, New York, October 1, 2012.

22. Pontifical Council for Justice and Peace, *Towards Reforming the International Financial and Monetary Systems*, conclusions.

23. *Caritas in veritate*, no. 67.

24. Cf. Pius XII, *Christmas Radio Message to the People of the Entire World*, December 24, 1944.

25. Cf. *Caritas in veritate*, no. 49.

26. Pontifical Council for Justice and Peace, *The Fight against Corruption*, Vatican City 2006, no. 10. Still on corruption, cf. Francis, *Homily*, June 17, 2014.

27. Benedict XVI, *Message for the World Day of Peace 2006*, no. 13.

28. Benedict XVI, *Message for the World Day of Peace 2007*, no. 15.

29. Benedict XVI, *Angelus*, Castel Gandolfo (Rome), July 29, 2007; cf. Holy See, *Intervention during the 3rd Session of the Preparatory Committee for the 9th Nuclear Non-Proliferation Treaty Review Conference*, New York, April 30, 2014.

30. John Paul II, *Message for the World Day of Peace 1990*, no. 9.

31. *Centesimus annus*, no. 40.

32. Benedict XVI, *Africae Munus*, no. 80.

33. Cf. World Bank, *Striking a Better Balance—The World Bank Group and Extractive Industries: The Final Report of the Extractive Industries Review*, September 17, 2004, executive summary.

34. Cf. *Gaudium et spes*, no. 74.

35. *Gaudium et spes*, no. 25.

36. Holy See, *Intervention at the Ministerial Conference on Nuclear Energy in the 21st Century*, Beijing, April 21, 2009.

37. *Catechism of the Catholic Church*, no. 1956.

38. Benedict XVI, *Address to the Bundestag*, apostolic journey to Germany, September 22, 2011.

39. Cf. John Paul II, *Address to the General Audience*, November 8, 1978, no. 3.

40. Benedict XVI, *Message to Participants in the 25th International Conference of the Pontifical Council for Health Care Workers*, November 15, 2010.

41. John Paul II, *Message for the World Day of Peace 1990*, no. 10.

42. Cf. *Compendium of the Social Doctrine of the Church*, chap. 4.

43. *Caritas in veritate*, no. 47.

44. Cf. *Compendium of the Social Doctrine of Church*, no. 186.

45. Cf. *Gaudium et spes*, no. 69.

46. Cf. John Paul II, *Message to the President of the Pontifical Council for Justice and Peace*, July 5, 2004.

47. Cf. UN-Habitat, *World Habitat Day 2011, Cities and Climate Change*, October 3, 2011, pp. 4 and 17.

48. John Paul II, *Message for the World Day of Peace 1990*, no. 10.

49. *Populorum progressio*, no. 65.

50. John Paul II, *Address to Participants in the Study Week on "Energy and Humanity" of the Pontifical Academy of Sciences*, November 14, 1980.

51. Cf. Paul VI, *Address for the Plenary Session of the Pontifical Academy of Sciences*, April 19, 1975.

52. *Caritas in veritate*, no. 69.

53. Cf. Benedict XVI, *Address to the New Ambassadors Accredited to the Holy See*, June 9, 2011.

54. Benedict XVI, *Message for the World Day of Peace 2010*, no. 10.

55. *Caritas in veritate*, no. 49.

56. Holy See, *Intervention at the 64th Session of the UN General Assembly, Second Committee on Item 53: Promotion of New and Renewable Sources of Energy*, New York, November 3, 2009.

57. Cf. John Paul II, *Message for the World Day of Peace 1990*, no. 6.

58. Cf. *Caritas in veritate*, no. 70.

59. Cf. Holy See, *Intervention at the 56th General Conference of the International Atomic Energy Agency*, Vienna, September 17, 2012, no. 6.

60. John Paul II, *Message for the World Day of Peace 1990*, no. 13.

61. *Centesimus annus*, no. 39.

62. Cf. *Compendium of the Social Doctrine of the Church*, nos. 369 and 375.

63. Ibid., no. 204.

64. Cf. ibid., no. 321.

65. Cf. ibid., no. 569.

66. John Paul II, *Address to the Participants in the Congress on Environment and Health*, March 24, 1997.

67. Benedict XVI, *Message for the World Day of Peace 2012*, no. 5.

Chapter 4

1. *Gaudium et spes*, no. 69.

2. John Paul II, *Message for the World Day of Peace 1990*, no. 10.

3. Idea promoted by the Focolari Movement, also recommended by many economists as a possible solution for sustainable development in the future; cf. John Paul II, *Address to the Bishops, Friends of the Focolari Movement*, February 12, 1999, no. 2; *Address to the Bishops of the Episcopal Conference of Brazil on Their "ad limina apostolorum" Visit*, November 26, 2002, no. 9.

Notes

4. Cf. Benedict XVI, *Address on the Occasion of the Meeting with the Civil Authorities at Westminster Hall,* September 17, 2010.

5. Holy See, *Intervention at the 64th Session of the UN General Assembly, Second Committee on Item 53: Promotion of New and Renewable Sources of Energy,* New York, November 3, 2009.

6. Cf. IEA, *Advantage Energy—Emerging Economies, Developing Countries and the Private-Public Sector Interface,* 2011, pp. 7ff.

7. Holy See, *Intervention at the 64th Session of the UN General Assembly, Second Committee on Item 53: Promotion of New and Renewable Sources of Energy,* New York, November 3, 2009; cf., *Intervention at the 13th General Conference of UNIDO - United Nations Industrial Development Organization,* Vienna, December 10, 2009.

8. About the damage caused by carbon dioxide, cf. John Paul II, *Address to Participants in the Study Week Organized by the Pontifical Academy of Sciences,* November 6, 1987, no. 2.

9. Cf. Pontifical Academy of Sciences, *Fate of Mountain Glaciers in the Anthropocene,* May 11, 2011.

10. Cf. *Caritas in veritate,* no. 50.

11. Cf. Intergovernmental Panel On Climate Change, *Renewable Energy Sources and Climate Change Mitigation,* Cambridge University Press, 2011, technical summary, p. 42.

12. Cf. Titus 2:11–12.

13. Benedict XVI, *Message Signed by Cardinal Tarcisio Bertone to the Director General of FAO on the Occasion of the World Water Day,* March 22, 2007.

14. John 6:12.

15. *Caritas in veritate,* no. 51.

16. John Paul II, *Message for the World Day of Peace 1990,* no. 13.

17. Pontifical Council for Justice and Peace, *Water, an Essential Element for Life—Contributions of the Holy See on Occasion of the World Water Forums* (Vatican City, 2013), 116.

18. UN, *Charter of the United Nations,* June 26, 1945, preamble.

19. UN, *The Universal Declaration of Human Rights*, December 10, 1948, art. 25.

20. Cf. *Gaudium et spes*, no. 69.

21. Cf. *Compendium of the Social Doctrine of the Church*, no. 152.

22. Cf. Africa Progress Panel, *Equity in Extractives—Stewarding Africa's Natural Resources for All*, 2013, pp. 55ff.

23. Cf. World Bank, *Striking a Better Balance—The World Bank Group and Extractive Industries: The Final Report of the Extractive Industries Review*, September 17, 2004, p. 3.

24. Including analyses of the lifecycle of the production process of the various biofuels in different contexts.

Chapter 5

1. Cf. *Compendium of the Social Doctrine of the Church*, no. 467; *Common Declaration of Pope Francis and the Ecumenical Patriarch Bartholomew I*, May 25, 2014, no. 6.

2. John Paul II, *Address to Gunkatsu Kano, Ambassador of Japan Accredited to the Holy See*, May 30, 2003.

3. Benedict XVI, *Angelus*, November 11, 2007.

4. John Paul II, *Message for the World Day of Peace 1990*, no. 13.

5. John Paul II, *Address to Participants in the Study Week on "Energy and Humanity" of the Pontifical Academy of Sciences*, November 14, 1980.

6. Cf. Benedict XVI, *Africae Munus*, no. 80.